Unfinished Easter

Sermons on the Ministry

HARPER'S MINISTERS PAPERBACK LIBRARY

Unfinished Easter

Sermons on the Ministry

David H. C. Read

Published in San Francisco by

HARPER & ROW, PUBLISHERS

New York, Hagerstown, San Francisco, London

FIRST EDITION

Designed by Michael A. Rogondino

Library of Congress Cataloging in Publication Data

Read, David Haxton Carswell.
   UNFINISHED EASTER.

   (Harper's ministers paperback library)
   1. Presbyterian Church—Sermons. 2. Sermons, American. I. Title.
BX9178.R367U53 1978   253′.2   77-20454
ISBN 0-06-066812-1

----

78 79 80 81 82 10 9 8 7 6 5 4 3 2 1

To
Charles Amstein
Paul Coleman

Partners in Ministry

Contents

Preface

The sub-title "Sermons on the Ministry" is not meant to
indicate that this book systematically covers all aspects of
Christian ministry today, nor that it was written with the
clergy in mind. What the reader will find is that the sermons deal with topics concerning the life and witness of
our churches today, and that they are more self-revealing
and autobiographical than this particular preacher has normally felt proper. I have been impressed that many today
seem to be asking: What does the preacher really believe
when not in the pulpit doing his job? or, more crudely:
What really makes him tick? So I have tried to express
what some of the truths I am expounding mean in my own
life and how I came to accept them.

Most of these sermons have been delivered on the National Radio Pulpit where the congregation envisaged is as
varied as the population of the United States. In this ministry I keep thinking, not only of the devout, deprived by age
or illness of normal church activity, but also of the agnostic,
the curious, and the uninterested who tune in by mistake.
So the potential audience includes the believer, the unbe-
liever, and the host of people who are looking for some
light in an increasingly complicated and confusing world.
The sermons are printed more or less as spoken into a
microphone—an instrument I love in the studio and detest
in the pulpit.

I trust that the "confessional" element will be found helpful rather than intrusive and that no minister, or anyone
else will imagine that I am saying: "Thus it can be and thus
it *should* be with you." The book is offered in the spirit of
the apostle when he said: "We preach not ourselves, but

Christ Jesus the Lord; and ourselves your servants for Jesus' sake" (2 Cor. 4:5). This is our ministry—your servants for Jesus' sake.

The quotations from the Bible in this book are from the King James Version, the New English Bible, and Today's English Version.

For inspiration and assistance in the preparation of these sermons, I want to thank correspondents near and far, and my gifted and patient secretary, Carolyn Mathis.

1

What Makes Me a Believer?

These sermons on one ministry are about religious convictions. Most sermons are, but in these I am going to be a little more personal than is my habit. I have in mind those who want to know what one particular preacher himself most deeply believes—and why. So this is not a series of theological lectures, expounding and defending the traditional beliefs of the churches, but an attempt to share and explore what such doctrines have come to mean to me today. They are a contribution to the lively discussion now going on—much to the surprise of the secularist establishment—about such matters as the spiritual dimension, salvation, the new birth, prayer, Christian ethics, eternal life, and even angels, devils, and the end of the world.

These things are being discussed today, not only in seminaries, but in homes, offices, airplanes, clubs, and cocktail parties. Bookstores are loaded with books on religious subjects, though these are seldom the production of the main-line churches, but more often the outpouring of theosophists, eastern mystics, evangelists, and adherents of the occult. A few years ago is was confidently predicted that we were moving toward a new scientific age where everything could be rationally explained, and people would no longer believe in the supernatural, the miraculous, or the transcendent. The very opposite has happened. This detached, objective, coldly rational age failed to show up, and all attempts to produce a "religionless Christianity" and to offer an easily digestible religion minus all that the so-called "modern mind" cannot accept have been left drooping in the void. This may not be a time of strong beliefs within the churches and synagogues, but a fantastic number of religious or quasi-religious beliefs abound in every sector of the American population. Today people are displaying a capacity for belief unequalled by recent generations in the shape of mystic cults, spiritism, divination, exorcism, clairvoyance, fortune telling, horoscopes, magic numbers, and every sort of superstition.

Recently, when I was preaching in another city the local newspaper carried a photograph of a benign, elderly clergyman whom I had never met, beneath which was the caption: "The Reverend David Read of Madison Avenue, New York." I pinned it on the bulletin board in my church office with the appended comment: "If you can believe this, you can believe anything." Later someone added the words popularized by one of the airlines: "You gotta believe!" It does indeed seem as if this must be today's motto: "You gotta believe!" Yet thoughtful people continue to ask why, and the more discriminating wonder whether the impulse to believe is not just a psychological reaction to a dangerous and confusing world. They are inclined to lump together all forms of religious belief, from the traditional creeds of the churches to the latest cults from California, as relatively harmless forms of escapism.

It's in this light that I want to risk making a personal confession of why I believe the major tenets of the Christian faith as it is expressed in the creeds and in the life and worship of the so-called "established" or "main-line" churches. In reply to the skeptic, I hold that religious belief is not a psychological quirk, but a reasonable, if adventurous, attitude of faith offering a clue to this mysterious universe and a dynamic of finding our way through the maze of everyday decisions. The more or less orthodox Christian convictions that I have come to hold don't necessarily make life any easier for me; in some ways they add to its load. But I have come to accept them because I believe them to be true. That belief is reinforced as I see them at work in other people whose lives reveal their truth more clearly than my own. In response to the current rash of rival beliefs and superstitions, I would maintain not only that there is a massive testimony to the truth and moral dynamic of a biblical tradition that will outlast most of the recent cults, but that the Bible contains insight enough to satisfy those with inquiring minds or restless spirits.

The late D. T. Niles, a native of Ceylon, where Christianity is a minority religion, once told some Western students: "Before you delve into all these questions about other religions why don't you first examine the tradition in which you were raised. Have you ever really studied the New Testament? Have you made up your mind about Jesus Christ?" It makes sense, doesn't it? The trouble is that many people assume they know all about Christianity, the Bible, and what the Church represents. So they write it off and go galloping off in some other direction. My plea is: "Hold it! Don't you think a faith that gave Western civilization its dynamic, inspired its greatest artists, produced its greatest writers, and nourished its astonishing saints might still be the way, the truth, and the life?"

Occasionally I come across people who are surprised that I still hold and defend the basic doctrines of orthodox Christianity. They seem to be saying: "You don't sound like a fanatic. You seem to have read a bit, travelled a bit, even thought a bit. Yet here you are professing belief in ideas and doctrines that I discarded in my adolescence. I suppose it must be your job. Ever since you decided to be a minister, I suppose you found yourself locked into an automatic acceptance of all these dogmas, and they just hang around your neck like that clerical collar." It's because of this assumption that the clergy have a vested interest in orthodoxy and have never really been exposed to the ravages of skepticism, or the attractions of rival religions, that I will be a little more personal here. I was once a layman, you know. All ministers were, in spite of the common delusion that we were born with clerical collars and imbibed the Apostles' Creed with our mother's milk. Though I was indeed baptized as an infant, I had more than an average dose of adolescent agnosticism. There was a time when I threw out most traditional beliefs and looked on them as rather boring relics of ancient religion. Real religion—or rather the living Christ—caught hold of me at a later stage, almost against my will. The call to the ministry came even later, and it was the most surprising thing that ever happened to me. It was neither in my family tradition nor the way I had conceived of my future.

If I were to give a straightforward answer to the question why I believe, I would first have to acknowledge my inheritance. Although some are apt to speak as if Christianity were their own private discovery, none of us arrive at faith entirely on our own. It is reported that Karl Barth, the greatest theologian of our time, was asked: "Why do you, with all your intellect and erudition, believe what Christianity teaches?" He replied with a twinkle in his eyes, "Because my mother told me." Of course he wasn't implying that he never questioned any of the traditions in which he was raised, but he was giving an honest answer about the way most of us have become believers. Our mothers often represent for us the Church universal and what they conveyed about belief in God was the basis of our future religion. What my mother told me is not necessarily true, but we need to be reminded that it isn't necessarily untrue. It's surprising how many people assume that if they can trace their beliefs back to a childhood influence, they have invalidated them. My mother also taught me that the world is round and that it's better to be unselfish than selfish, and I haven't seen any reason yet to think she was wrong.

We are perhaps at a point now of giving a little more thought to the value of our religious traditions. Having been through a period when history was apt to be ignored, traditions despised, and enormous importance given to the new and the now, we may be a little more ready to concede that our ancestors were not totally ignorant and misguided in their convictions. We are beginning to realize that progress in scientific knowledge doesn't necessarily mean progress in moral or spiritual understanding, that the generation that landed a man on the moon is not necessarily wiser, kinder, or more spiritually aware than that which produced Isaiah, Augustine, Mozart, or Abraham Lincoln. So I don't despise the fact that my religious beliefs first came to me from my ancestors. Nor am I disposed to doubt them on the grounds that, if I had been born at another place or another time I might have been a Buddhist, a Moslem, or a Marxist. I just accept what happened, and am grateful.

I am grateful because in the end I came to a personal conviction that, in essence, what my mother told me is true. After exposing myself to the influence of skeptical writers, and such study of other faiths as I was able to make, it gradually dawned on me that the Christian faith can satisfy the mind at least as fully as any alternative explanation of this strange adventure of human life, and the mysterious universe around us. I am not saying that I was argued into faith; I don't believe anyone ever is. But I discovered the hard way that what some call a leap of faith leaves one with at least as satisfying a view of life as any rival philosophy. It also became clear to me that, in the end, every conviction about human life—Christian, Jewish, Moslem, agnostic, Marxist, atheist, existentialist—is an act of faith. It is as difficult to prove there is no God as to prove that there is. I am willing to accept the verdict of the experts on things that can be scientifically proved, but in matters of ultimate belief about the purpose or meaning of life, or what is good or beautiful, no such proof is possible. We all act on faith. And, in spite of all who call it into question, I still find the Christian view of the meaning of life and how it should be lived more satisfying than any other.

But I've not yet explained what really makes me believe. It isn't merely tradition, or its appeal to my mind.

Something had to happen. There are people who drift along with a vague attachment to the religion of their forefathers, but who really couldn't be called believers. They might claim to be Christians in a negative kind of way, meaning that they are not atheists or adherents of any other faith. You might say that they sail through life with a kind of side-bet on God, hoping toward the end that there may, after all, be a heaven to receive them. But you could hardly say that, in any real sense, Christ was either Savior or Lord of their lives. And there are also people who have no serious doubts about the truth of the Christian faith. It generally makes sense to them, but they are not aware of any vital change in their lives being worked by the Spirit of Christ. Again, something else must happen. But what is it?

We must begin to talk about some kind of invasion from the other side. Ultimately all vital belief in God or the experience of the Christian life is the result of being gripped by him. The New Testament seldom describes the experience of becoming a Christian as a quest, and never as an achievement. Men and women simply testify that somewhere along the line they were captivated by the living Christ. It's the same in the Old Testament. The prophets and kings, as well as the ordinary people, became aware of the presence of the sovereign God and responded to his call. None of these people, even Moses or Paul, ever spoke of his own brilliant discovery of the divine. Each spoke in his own way of an encounter in which he became vividly aware that God was addressing him, and each responded through belief. After all, I don't profess to believe in my dearest friend simply because someone told me he existed, or because I am intellectually convinced that there is such a person. I believe in him because in one way or another he has revealed himself to me, and I responded.

So it is between me and God. I believe in him because he has met me. I don't mean that in my case there was one shattering, overwhelming religious experience in which God exploded into my life. There have been what you might call decisive, illuminating, or even overwhelming moments. But on the whole it has been a gradual process.

And all the time it has not been a matter of my strivings, my special gifts, or my religious capacity, but of God's approach to me, his disclosure, his leadings, and, above all, what I have learned to call his grace. In the end it is not my inheritance, my mind, or even my experience that makes me a believer. It is the love of God. To live, as far as possible, within this love is to be beyond the reach of ultimate skepticism. This is why the short-lived cult of the "Death of God" made no impression on the real believers. You can't tell a man or woman who lives in daily contact with the living God that, in fact, there's no one there.

I want to discuss later some of the dimensions of faith, some of our difficulties, some of our limitations, and some of the unexplored territories awaiting the believer. So far I have just been trying to answer the basic question: What makes you a believer? I am aware that some may say: "That's all very well for you. What if I have never had such an experience?" There is indeed a mystery about why some seem to find belief easy while others find it next to impossible. I can only say that "easy belief" is not necessarily the deepest kind of faith, and that I cannot believe that God withholds all knowledge of himself from anyone. So much depends on whether or not we really want to know him. I remember the words Pascal (Pensés VII 553) heard when he was in doubt and near despair: "You would not be seeking me unless you had already found me." To want to believe, to want to know God, may be your answer. If you are really searching, could it be that God has prompted your search? You and I could only become real to each other if I wanted to know you and you wanted to know me. I honestly believe that God wants to know you. Do you want to know him? Honestly?

O God, we would now be still so that thou canst speak. May this moment be for us all a time when belief wakens in the soul. There is much to make us hesitate, much to make us doubt, much to make us confused. Lord, we believe. Help our unbelief through Jesus Christ thy Son. Amen.

2

What I Mean by Religion

Like most people I once had a religious aunt. She was really a great aunt, a sister of my grandmother. She was known in the family as religious because she was not only a fervent churchgoer, but conducted morning prayers every day in her home. She also provided my brother and me at regular intervals with what were then known as "improving" books. Some of these were quite lurid tales, which we learned to read without paying much attention to the moral lessons in the last chapters. Others we tolerated for the sake of thrilling and gory illustrations of such stories as Daniel in the lions' den or David cutting off Goliath's head. The point is that this aunt was always known as religious while her sister didn't seem to fall into that category. It was only later that I perceived that my grandmother, who said little about religion and regaled us with fairy tales or adventures from her youth, was in many ways far more what I would now call religious than my aunt. To be with her was somehow to absorb unconsciously what it means to "do justly and to love mercy and to walk humbly with our God" (Mic. 6:8).

Religious is thus a slippery word. I wonder how you would answer the question: Are you religious? If you thought the question meant: Are you known for your devout habits? Are you easily shocked? Are you liable to sound off about your beliefs on all occasions? then you might want to answer, "No." But if you thought the question meant: Do you acknowledge a God, or at least some kind of spiritual dimension to your life? then you might want to say, "Yes." The chances are that many today would be inclined to answer: "Not very," or "Yes—in my own way."

It seems important to me for anyone talking about religion to clear up this ambiguity. At this point in our nation's story the question of what is meant by real, or genuine, religion has become more acute than ever. For not only are we confronted by a bewildering variety of religions, new and old, with demanding and often contradictory claims, but we have passed through a national moral crisis in which opposite conclusions were drawn about the influence of religion.

On the one hand millions have awakened to the truth that the most powerful nation in the world cannot survive by virtue of its material strength, abundant resources, political skills, or technological brilliance unless it is nourished by moral and spiritual convictions such as have been traditionally generated by a genuine belief in God—the God of justice and mercy. For them it is clear that the time is ripe for a revival of prayer, worship, and religious convictions and for a repudiation of the apathy and moral relativism into which we have been sinking. They see a great need for a deep and widespread revival of religious belief.

On the other hand there are many who draw opposite conclusions from the shattering events of recent years. They question the validity of religion in the modern world, and think of it as the playground of the intellectually idle, or (still worse) as a smoke screen behind which the greedy and the power-hungry pursue their wicked ways. They point to the number of religious movements that were alive in the land at the very time when moral standards were slipping and basic rights and liberties were being threatened. According to them, the last thing we need is a revival of this sentimentality, superstition, and hypocrisy.

It is in answer to this division of opinion that I want to offer my definition of true religion. I believe that the time has come for a nationwide renewal of faith in God, for an awakening to the only source of meaning and direction for a confused and disillusioned generation. I am convinced that nothing on the horizon now, East or West, offers genuine hope for humanity short of a living contact with the world of the spirit that real religion alone can give. But I would underline the word *real*, for I readily admit that unreal, bogus, and frivolous religion abound in our day and add to our confusion and despair. It's time that it was generally understood that all religion is not necessarily good. Modern Americans are so conditioned to be tolerant and respectful toward all that is popularly known as "religious" that we have forgotten the truth behind the old axiom that "the corruption of the best is the worst." It is because, in my view, real religion is the best thing in life, that its perversion is so damaging and vicious. Jesus, you remember, did not hesitate to denounce phony religion, and reserved his most violent denunciations for the very people who were popularly considered exceptionally religious.

In presidential elections in the United States, "the religious issue" sometimes surfaces. This is nearly always resented by those who want to draw a sharp dividing line between religion and politics and speak of the impenetrable wall between church and state. No reasonable person wants religious bigotry or sectarian rivalry to intrude into the political process. But when I am told that a candidate's religious convictions are irrelevant, and that we have no right to know anything about them, I wonder what concept of religion is being expressed. A religion that has no effect whatever on a person's political views, moral decisions, or philosophy of life is certainly not the religion of the Bible. Anyone who declares that his religion will not in any way affect his attitudes toward the great questions of our day, or his behavior in public life, is implying that religion is a private predilection like stamp-collecting or mountaineering

with no vital influence on his life. I have no desire to
support a candidate simply because he belongs to the same
religious denomination as I do, but I do want to know what
kind of convictions underlie his judgments and behavior.

We all know how religion can be exploited on the
political scene, and history has disclosed notorious examples
of what could be called fraudulent piety. Yet in the presidential election of 1976, both candidates, when asked, gave
straightforward witness to their religious convictions. Mr.
Carter declared that he was a Christian believer and that
prayer was important in his daily life. Mr. Ford disclosed
on one occasion that he had the habit of repeating every
night the Bible verse: "Trust in the Lord with all thine
heart, and lean not unto thine own understanding. In all thy
ways acknowledge him, and he shall direct thy paths"
(Prov. 3:6).

That verse is a good example of what I mean by the
word *religion*. At the root of any genuine religion, there is a
basic humility, an acknowledgment that we are not autono-
mous. "Trust in the Lord . . . and lean not unto thine own
understanding." We are not our own boss, our own judge,
our own God. To be religious means that we realize we are
both dependent and responsible—dependent on the God
who brought us into being, and responsible in all things to
him. In real religion humanity itself is likewise dependent
and responsible. Unlike the humanists, the believer finds
his authority and his sanctions in a God who is more than
humanity with a capital *H*, one who is the source of all
meaning and the ultimate judge "unto whom all hearts are
open, all desires known, and from whom no secrets are
hid" (Book of Common Prayer: Collect for Purity). To trust
in the Lord with all our hearts instead of leaning on our
own understanding doesn't mean despising our thought
processes, or calling a halt to the great story of human
invention and discovery. It means that we realize the limits
of human understanding and that we are ultimately dependent on the grace and guidance of God. To be religious is
to make the decisive choice as to whether or not there is a

power beyond ourselves on whom we depend, from whom
we gain insight, and whom we can utterly trust.

This is the basic question of all true religion. Once in
the army another chaplain and I became engaged in a
prolonged debate with a couple of informed and deter-
mined atheists. We happened to be in a prison camp, so we
had plenty opportunity for frequent and uninhibited discussion—and more time for it than any of us really wanted. So
we explored our differences in a lengthy, honest, and good-
tempered exercise that we had not then learned to call a
"confrontation." I remember reaching a point when one of
the atheists finally said something like this: "I believe in the
end the main difference between us is the question of
humility. I'm damned if I want to acknowledge any boss
beyond myself or the human race." At that point my col-
league and I felt there was little more to be said, but, faced
with the humility of such a confession, we could hardly feel
any pride in winning the argument.

Our friend had indeed touched the center of real religion. It doesn't matter how religious a man or a woman
seems to be, if there is no real humility in them they are
not religious at all. When Jesus said: "Blessed are the meek:
for they shall inherit the earth," he was indicating precisely
this abdication of our claim to lean entirely on our own
understanding and to be our own boss. He was commending humility as the key to the fullness of life. Where it is
lacking, no matter what people profess, men and women
succumb to the pride or "hubris" that Greek dramatists
perceived to be the fatal flaw leading to all human tragedy.
And an entire people can be carried away on a wave of
illusions about human omnipotence and perfectibility. What
better advice could be given to anyone to whom much
power is entrusted than to "trust in the Lord with all thy
might and lean not unto thine own understanding." Real
religion takes that seriously—and not as a passing thought
for Sunday morning. It's the note that rings through the
Bible. In the Old Testament the standard of judgment upon
nations and individuals is not their success, their efficiency,

or even their wisdom, but whether or not they "walked humbly with their God." In the New Testament, which tells the story of the humility and self-emptying of the Son of God, the Word we hear is: "Let this mind be in you which was also in Christ Jesus (Phil. 2:5). . . . You are not your own. . . . You are bought with a price" (I Cor. 6:19,20). What I mean by religion is freedom from illusions about our own understanding and our human self-sufficiency, and a determination to walk humbly with God.

The text in the Book of Proverbs goes on: "In all thy ways acknowledge him, and he shall direct thy paths" (3:6). With these words any notion that religion is something that can be confined to special occasions or to certain aspects of our lives is demolished. What I mean by religion is this integrity of life of which the Bible speaks from beginning to end. "In all thy ways acknowledge him. . . ." We are not told "on Sunday mornings acknowledge him," or "acknowledge him with a conventional reference at the end of a speech, or with an invocation before a public dinner, or when you are asked by a pollster if you believe in God." "In all thy ways acknowledge him. . . ." This is where we reach the vital distinction between real religion and the bogus. Real religion has an integrity that covers the whole of life, and leaves no room for neutral or secular areas where the thought of God is excluded.

For a national leader, "in all thy ways" means a religion that is operative, not just in public references to God, but in the council chambers where decisions are made. (I remember that Adolf Hitler seldom concluded any major speech without an invocation of the almighty.) But this definition of religion is not given us so that we can criticize the behavior of those in power. It comes home to all of us. "In all thy ways. . . ." Are there any areas of life where religion really plays no part? What's the meaning of that phrase you often hear: "Let's keep religion out of this"? Can we think of major or minor decisions we have made, in which there was no acknowledgment of God?

Real religion has an integrity, a "wholeness," and a life

that is integrated, made one by an overriding loyalty and dedication. The Bible speaks of this total loyalty to God, which is why it deals with so much that is not normally thought of as religious at all. The Word of God in the Bible speaks through the marketplace, the wedding feast, the battlefield, the law courts, the health services, and domestic and foreign policies, just as much as through the worship of the sanctuary. Jesus, in the blazing integrity of his life, carried his good news about God into every corner and to every kind of person, religious or irreligious, with such a total dedication that it has been said that he abolished religion altogether. A few years ago the phrase "religionless Christianity" was being bandied about and caused some confusion in church circles. What it really meant was that to follow Jesus is to follow him everywhere, not just in those sections of life labeled "religious." Real religion is not one concern among many, a private indulgence like a taste for caviar or antique furniture. It's a pervasive attitude toward the whole of life—a mind-set, a heart-set that affects everything we say or do—or it is not real at all.

And that attitude is trust: trust in the living God, trust in a Lord who offers his guidance and his grace through the hazards and the darkness of the road we tread. Trust isn't easy. As Jesus pointed out, we are not naturally humble enough to yield our egos to the God who made us. We resist his claim on every aspect of our lives; we do not have the total integrity of life that Jesus both taught and lived; and trust in the grace and guidance of God seems to many of us harder as the years go by. This is why I believe we still need the strengthening power of those activities that are normally called "religious"—prayer, worship, and the fellowship of the Church. We don't call these "religious activities" in the sense that religion is sealed up within the walls of an organized church. I find it necessary to set aside time and energy for "religious exercises" just to reinforce a trust in God that can carry through to every part of daily life. I believe that those who pause to acknowledge God, week by week, surrounded by companions in the faith and the company of heaven, find it easier, consciously or unconsciously, to acknowledge him at home, in business, at play, in social contacts, and in daily decisions.

This, then, is what I mean by religion—the humility that leans on God for the direction and guidance of our life; the integrity that acknowledges him in all our ways; and a basic trust that he alone knows the way we should go and can provide the inner strength, forgiveness, and refreshment that all of us need. This, to me, is basic religion. And I respect it under whatever label it may be found.

Lord, help us to know thee more surely as the God who is with us day by day and night by night. May thy presence guide and refresh us in every task, so that all our decisions may be prompted by thy spirit, all our trials opened to thy grace, and all our joys consecrated by thy love. In the name of Jesus Christ keep us from saying, "Lord, Lord," and being disobedient to thy will. Amen.

3

O Church, with All Thy Faults, I Love Thee Still

For a long time criticizing and castigating the Christian Church has been a popular pastime. Ever since the Church ceased to be a little network of Christian communities struggling for survival in the Roman Empire and became a formidable institution in the Western world, it has been the target of attack by wits, cynics, and moralists in every generation. If these attacks are not so vehement and prominent in our day and our part of the world, the reason is probably that few now think of the Church as a very powerful or influential institution. "How many divisions has the Pope?" asked Stalin, voicing the contempt of the mighty for the militarily powerless. In the democracies, people are apt to ask: "How much political clout has the Church?" and the answer would certainly be, "Not nearly so much as some years ago." The Church today is in much more danger of being ignored than being attacked. In recent years, for instance, the press has given little space to church news beyond the stereotypes of liberal-conservative controversy or local trivialities. Critics seldom bother to castigate an institution that seems to be relatively powerless in our secular society.

Yet, beneath the surface, the rumbling and grumbling

go on. Each new generation thinks it has discovered for the first time a yawning gap between Jesus and the Church that bears his name. Every time I hear a student express an admiration for Jesus and a dislike of his Church, I remember my own teenage point of view. I was thrilled by Jesus and bored with his Church, attracted by the figure in the Gospels and repelled by the religious machinery that claimed to represent him. I devoured the theories of Bernard Shaw, who wrote scathingly about how Paul had turned Christianity into "Crosstianity" and created an institution that betrayed nearly every ideal represented by the simple carpenter of Nazareth. Somehow the church as a place of worship had lost any appeal it had when I was a child, and what went on in it had little connection with the things that were arousing my adolescent interest. The Church as part of the national scene looked to me like a conspiracy of clergymen chiefly occupied in denouncing the favorite amusements of ordinary men and women.

So I am bound to retain some sympathy for the complaints that I hear today. From what is being said I get the impression that it is the organizational aspect of the Church that gives most offense today. It's no longer possible to denounce the Church for its conspicuous wealth or arrogance or to complain that it wields a crushing power over the habits and pleasures of the whole population. With some exceptions one could say that this kind of church no longer exists. But the image of the Church as an organization, as a kind of religious corporation much more occupied with the ecclesiastical machinery than with the life of the spirit, remains. The intense religious fervor of our day, the search for vivid spiritual experience, the interest in meditation and mysticism, the enthusiasm for prophetic figures, and the quest for the esoteric and the occult have not led to a stampede into the established churches or a growth in their membership. It seems to be taken for granted that, generally speaking, the real religious action is not in the churches.

Even among those who are not caught up in these

forms of excitement, there is a strong resistance to the claims of the Church. Many people make a clear distinction between personal religious conviction and membership in a local church. I regularly meet the wedding guest who confides to me at the reception something like this: "I liked your service today. You know, I'm not much of a churchgoer, but I believe in God and try to do the right thing. That's what matters, isn't it?" Behind this sort of remark I hear the Church being brushed aside as an optional activity for Christians who happen to like getting mixed up in its activities. Some people feel strongly that membership in a church would add nothing to one's religious experience, and would, in fact, involve the hypocrisy of pretending to believe much more than one really does. Some people are just allergic to joining anything these days and particularly resent the idea of linking their religion to some particular denomination.

Since I am confessing my own faith, instead of giving you the textbook answers to these complaints and possible misunderstandings, let me try to explain why I found myself, without any parental compulsion, eventually drawn into the Church, and why, after many years in its ministry, I can honestly say, "O Church, with all thy faults, I love thee still." (Incidentally, when I inquired around to see if anyone knew where this phrase came from I found most people were inclined to attach some girl's name to the phrase "with all thy faults, I love thee still." Others thought it originated in a popular song. I finally traced it down to the eighteenth-century English poet, William Cowper, who wrote in a moment of passionate patriotism: "England, with all thy faults, I love thee still. . . ." Whatever the reference, I think we all know the feeling—and it certainly expresses my attachment to the Christian Church.)

I've already mentioned how little the Church appealed to me in my teens. That is natural enough when I was going through the agnostic stage, but it continued after I had become a convinced Christian believer. For my faith came alive through the influence of evangelical groups, and

things like camp-meetings where the Gospel was presented
as a very personal appeal from Christ, in surroundings that
attracted my particular age-group. Compared to the excitement and fervor of receiving Christ as Lord and Savior in
this context, the Church seemed a rather drab and lifeless
institution. I was not the slightest bit interested in church
assemblies, committees, pronouncements, and reports. It
seemed to me then, as it obviously does to many today, that
being a Christian was one thing, and attaching oneself to a
church was quite another. What, then, led me to change my
mind, and how did a genuine love for the Church emerge
over the years?

I think the change began when I realized that the
Church was more than the local building with all that went
on within its walls, and more than the institution that
loomed over the nation like a kind of moral and religious
police force. As I began to study the Bible I found that from
the very beginning Christians found themselves part of a
community they called the Church. There was no suggestion
in the New Testament that a man or woman could decide
to be a Christian and then make a later decision whether or
not to be a member of this community. On the day of
Pentecost suddenly the Church was there, and those who
believed were added to it. Believing, baptism, and joining
the Church were apparently all aspects of the same event. It
dawned on me that, unlike most other religions, Christianity
is a Church and that there is no such thing as a lone and
isolated Christian. So what I was receiving from the groups
that influenced me I was also receiving from the Church.

From that thought it wasn't far to the understanding
that the very Gospel I had heard and received was not the
invention of the men I heard it from, but had been handed
down from the earliest days within the community known
as the Church. I realized that the early religious instruction
I received from my parents was also from the same source.
In fact one can say that most of us met the Church for the
first time in the person of our mother. I discovered that in
the Bible the Church is called the Body of Christ. This must

mean that Christ expresses himself and continues his work on earth through this community, just as his human body was the instrument for his mission long ago in the Holy Land. How can one not love this Church, so intimately related to Christ himself? I began to understand how passionately a man or woman could learn to care for, and work for, a company of people spread across the centuries and across the world, which may well evoke the title "Mother Church." I remember being surprised to find in the writings of John Calvin the statement that no one can be a Christian without being born in the womb of the Church and nourished at her breast.

All this may perhaps sound a bit mystical and detached from the reality of the church we know round the corner. It isn't really, for the local congregation, consisting of people worshiping together and trying to serve Christ, is the motherchurch in action where we live. In the same way the affiliation of the local church with its denomination and ecumenical councils of various kinds indicates that its members are part of a worldwide community that represents the Body of Christ on earth. Of course, as soon as you stop thinking about the Church in the resounding words of the creeds as "one holy, catholic, and apostolic," and look at the life and activity of the local church, the denominations, and the councils, you can't help seeing its human weaknesses and betrayals. But that is how it must be until the struggling Church on earth becomes the Church triumphant in heaven.

Once one understands that the church we know is just people—people who have responded to Jesus Christ with varying degrees of intensity—the notion of a perfect institution or ideal community is bound to disappear. So I learned to be more tolerant of the local church. Among other things I realized that a church must consist of all kinds of people, of different ages, and varying occupations, and that, therefore, I couldn't expect to feel as comfortable in it as I was with my own contemporaries in the camps and gatherings. I have learned to love the rich diversity of a living church. When people say that there is more real fellowship in their

club or their favorite bar than in a church, I want to reply
that while you choose your friends in such places, you don't
choose your fellow church-members. They are given you.
And sometimes your common bond in Christ is the only
thing that could hold you together.

"O Church, with all thy faults. . . ." Of course I know
the faults: anyone who works daily within the structure
knows them better than any outside critic. This is so true
that the most vociferous complaints about the church today
come from within. It's about time, I believe, for the moan-
ing and groaning, the stream of complaints and criticisms, to
give way to a new affirmation of our deep love for the
Church we serve. There has been altogether too much mud-
slinging, not only at the hierarchies and councils, but at the
local parish. It's encouraging to note that in a recent survey
of ministers, chiefly concerning salaries, it emerged that the
vast majority of them, in spite of very low average recom-
pense, declared that they found satisfaction and enjoyment
in their work. In other words, they love the Church of Jesus
Christ, even in the concrete form of the local institution.
Why? Let me give my own answer.

First, I love the Church as the Body of Christ on earth,
the community that has given me birth as a Christian, and
in which alone I find communion with fellow Christians in
every land and with the saints in heaven. To me there
would be a fearful arrogance in saying: "I love Christ, but
loathe the company of disciples he created to proclaim his
Gospel and carry on his ministry."

Second, I love the Church in its visible and human
manifestation in a local congregation. I am moved by the
worship of a mixed group of people of all ages seeking to
express their sense of God's presence and to respond to the
Word and the Sacraments of Christ. I am touched by what
one can only call the signs of grace, whereby lives are
changed, friendships formed, forgiveness experienced, and
children nurtured in the faith. I marvel at the diverse ways
in which church-members respond to the call to minister to
others in the name of Jesus. I am excited by the strength of

the spiritual ties that hold together people of widely different temperaments and opinions. And I rejoice that, in spite
of all failures and follies, the Holy Spirit does offer in a
living Church the supportive fellowship that we all so sore-
ly need. I'll never forget the young woman who became a
member of the Church for the first time shortly before she
was stricken with cancer. From her hospital bed she said to
me with a smile: "I never knew before what it meant to
have the backing of a church." The more a church offers
such backing, the more I love it.

Lastly, I love the Church because, with all her faults,
Christ has chosen this company of people to be the instrument of his love on earth and opened her doors wide to
receive all who respond to his Gospel. The Church may
limp and sputter through this era of change and confusion,
but where else is there such a worldwide fellowship of
hope, such a community of faith, and such a reservoir of
love? And always, out ahead, where the world finds chaos
and darkness, I hear the hallelujahs of the Church
triumphant.

*We bring to thee our thanks, Lord God, for the great
company of the faithful whom thou has bound together in
the communion of thy Church; for those who serve and
worship here on earth; and those who rejoice with thee in
heaven. Revive the churches of our day with the fire of thy
spirit, and draw into them all who walk alone and are
afraid; through Jesus Christ our Lord. Amen.*

4

My Adventures and Misadventures with the Bible

It must be rather puzzling for those who are not Christian believers that our faith seems to be tied up with a collection of books known as the Bible. Most people think of religion as a belief in God and contact with him today, and wonder why we should be dependent on writings that have come down to us from the distant past. No other religion, except Judaism and Islam, makes such a fuss about a sacred book. The cults of mysticism and meditation that flourish today offer vivid religious experience that isn't normally related to any sacred Scripture. Many assume we can find our way around in the field of religion without reference to the thoughts and experiences of people who lived hundreds of years ago.

The simplest response is that Christianity, like Judaism, is an historical religion. It offers a communion with God today that is based on something that happened in our world. For Christians the greatest happening was the appearance of Jesus, and our faith depends on who he was, what he said, what he did, and what happened to him. And this we learn from the Bible, the record not only of his life, death, and resurrection, but the story of the Jewish people to whom he belonged, and the Church that he caused to appear. For Christians, then, the Bible is the anchor that moors us to the facts about the Lord we worship and seek to serve.

But I don't want to offer you this kind of textbook answer to the question of the Bible, or to succumb to the temptation of elaborating it with other explanations of its place in the Christian Church. In these talks about the ministry I'm trying to express what certain familiar Christian ideas and practices have come to mean to me over the years, and why I'm in the business of passing them on—in other words, what makes this particular person tick? So, instead of concentrating on the authority of the Bible and why we ought to read it, I will give an account of what I'm calling my own adventures and misadventures with the Scriptures.

Adventures and misadventures—that may seem a curious choice of words. For some, adventure is the last thing they associate with the Bible. Lying up there on the shelf it looks thoroughly tame, dull, and domesticated, part of the furniture of a conventional home. For others misadventure is a rather shocking word to use about a sacred book. You have misadventures with a rollicking companion, but not with your grandmother. Yet I stand by both words from my own experience and that of thousands of others, past and present. Some of the greatest movements in history sprang from an individual's venture with the Bible—such as Augustine's, Luther's, or Wesley's—and today it's not hard to find young people whose lives are being turned upside down by their encounter with this book. As for the misadventures—how else would you describe the appalling results of Bible-readings that have led to massacres and witch-hunts or the excesses of those who claim to find in Daniel or Revelation an exact timetable for imminent events or a date for the end of the world.

If I dig back to childhood memories I find that the Bible first appealed to me as a kind of adventure book. Quite apart from questions of religion, I feel that children today who never heard the Bible stories have been terribly

deprived. Those of us who were lucky enough to have the
world of the Bible opened up by sensible parents or teach-
ers, and to be given illustrated selections rather than fat
little black books with tiny print, remember thrilling to the
adventures of Moses, Samuel, David, Daniel, and Paul, and
being gripped by the haunting tales in the Gospels. We may
smile as we think back to our happy acceptance of stories
that now raise many questions in our sophisticated minds.
Our first misadventures with the Bible may have occurred if
we were later led to believe that the Bible stories belonged
with the fairy tales of childhood. But now I realize that I
was learning something that in our adult years we easily
forget: the Bible is about real people and what happened to
them rather than a collection of abstract religious truths.
Through these stories a child absorbs the precious truth that
life is an adventure story, an adventure for each one of us
and for the human race, an adventure in which God plays
the leading role. That's worth any amount of fact-feeding
and moralizing.

I have to confess that after these childhood years the
Bible didn't play a large part in my daily life. It was something I heard in church or was forced to memorize in
school. I shared youthful suspicion of people we called
"Bible-bashers," and dimly felt that the Scriptures were
really the preserve of clergymen and others who found
them a useful source for sermonizing. As I began to develop a taste for literature, the cadences of the King James
Version actually awakened in me a sense of wonder and
adventure. But I can also remember at this time the furtive
schoolboy discovery, passed on in whispers, that there were
actually in the Bible some very naughty four-letter words.
You might call this our first misadventure with the Bible,
except for the fact that one was learning that the Bible is
indeed a most outspoken book and by no means as solemn
and prudish as those who seem to read it most avidly.

Looking back, I date my real misadventures with the
Bible to the period when I swung from one extreme to the
other in estimating its authority. These were my adolescent

years. Initially, I fell in with those writers and speakers whose delight was, as they put it, to debunk the Bible. It seemed quite devastating to me that the Bible had been put together over a great number of years by people of varied skills and edited by many different hands. For some reason the discovery of the literary and historical roots of the Bible seemed to me to rob it of all claims to divine revelation. Similarly, the fact that Bible writers wrote in the idiom of their day and accepted the science of their day seemed to invalidate anything they had to say about God or human behavior. Even the emphasis of H. G. Wells in his *Outline of History* on the tiny extent of the land of Palestine and the modest dimensions of Solomon's Temple somehow became a reason for scorning this book. What fun it was to dwell on the discrepancies in the various accounts, the anthropomorphic pictures of God (how we liked to hurl that word around, forgetting that there is no other way for a human being to attempt to talk of God in human terms), and the trick question about where Cain found his wife.

I call this a misadventure, for what a tragedy it is that a boy or girl can be led to believe that because the Bible has been written and put together by real people, and not by some celestial machine, it cannot be a spiritual and moral power or the vehicle of the Word of God himself. I am immensely grateful that while still in this mood of rebellion against conventional veneration of the Bible I came under the spell of people, mostly my own age or slightly older, who used the Bible to speak to me about Jesus Christ. Somehow as I listened to them my previous doubts and denials fell into the background, for they were talking about a living Lord who was addressing me—of all people—through these Biblical stories and sayings.

For a time, then, I set aside the literary and historical questions, and just let the Bible speak to my needs as I sought to know and to follow Christ. I was amazed how stories and sayings I had often heard before sprang to life and seemed to speak directly to me. Someone once said, "I believe the Bible because it *finds* me." That was what was happening to me, and I still think it's the greatest adventure anyone can have with the Bible. The misadventure at that time was that most of those I was listening to insisted that the whole Bible—from cover to cover, as they were fond of saying—was divinely dictated and thus preserved from any human error or the normal vicissitudes of literary productions. Any attempt to understand the differences in style and backgrounds of the various books was ruled out, and ingenious theories were offered to explain such difficulties as the obvious differences between the morality of the Book of Judges and that of the Sermon on the Mount, or the varied accounts that are given by different writers of the same event. I began to notice that in practice those who insisted on this theory of Biblical inspiration operated with a comparatively small selection from the Scriptures and freely used allegory to make every text yield the doctrine they wanted to impart. It began to dawn on me that one didn't need to have this rigid, mechanical view of the authority of the Bible for it to bring the Word of God to me.

So my next great adventure with the book was when I discovered that I was not locked into deciding whether it was purely human or purely divine. Just as the Christian faith rests on the paradox that Jesus Christ is both fully human and fully divine, so I learned to approach the Bible. It was a release to be able to accept fully the human personalities of the different authors with their natural limitations and prejudices, and to allow competent scholars to teach me how the books were put together. And it was a joy to realize that a thoroughly humanized Bible had in no way lost its power to convey the Word of God himself. Questions of authorship, dating, editing, and historical background fell into place; what mattered was what the Holy Spirit is saying to us through these writings. So to this day, when I study a biblical passage for my own use or to prepare a sermon, I look on these historical and literary questions as preliminaries to enable me to hear better what God is saying now.

The greatest adventure anyone can have with the Bible

is when the Spirit of God makes a verse, a passage, or a whole book come alive, and we are confronted with the claims of the living God and nourished by the deepest truths of the Gospel. Lots of other books have been helpful to me as I have sought to understand, to accept, and to live by this Gospel, but there is not one that has for me the authority of the Bible. There I find the original witness of prophets and apostles to what God has done to create and sustain a company of believers, and to rescue humanity from destruction and despair. The other books ultimately derive their power from what the Bible has recorded. It has the extraordinary capacity to speak in a new way to each succeeding generation. Our adventure with it really begins when we forget all about the theories that explain its power, both the foolish attacks and the equally foolish defenses to which it has been subjected, and just let it speak. No one has a right to say, "You can't expect to find any truth for today in this ancient collection of myths and fantasies"; or, "Before you start reading you must accept my theory about its inspiration and infallibility." In the words of the last chapter of the last book of the Bible: "Let him that is athirst come. And whosoever will, let him take the water of life freely" (Rev. 27:17).

I hope I have shown, however inadequately, why the Bible has been a unique interpreter of life for me and is integral to the faith by which I live. Through adventures and misadventures it has become for me an anchor and a launching pad. It is an anchor in the sense that, time and again, it recalls me to the vision of God, to the only true perspective in which to live, and to the claims and promises of the Christian Gospel. It is an anchor when we are exposed to gales and squalls of doubt, distress, and despair, and when even the churches drift off course and neglect the priorities of the Gospel. I am convinced that in the testing days ahead of us it will be Christians and churches nourished by the Bible that will know how to endure with faith and joy. So the Bible is also for me as a preacher the anchor on which I depend.

But it's more than an anchor; the Bible can also be thought of as a launching pad. Every generation finds in this book the Word that sends us soaring off to new discoveries and adventures of the spirit. When I prepare a sermon, turning to a familiar text again and again, I find that it's not so familiar after all. If I give the Spirit a chance to speak afresh, the Bible passage sends me off in quite unexpected directions. As the old Puritan said, God has more and more light continually to break out of His Word. The same thing happens when a group studies a passage together. In an astonishing way new thoughts and challenges are generated by sharing the text.

What has come home to me as I prepared this talk is not just how much I have owed to the Bible through the different stages of my life, but how much there still lies in it for me to discover. I could well use Paul's words: "My friends, I do not reckon myself to have got hold of it yet. All I can say is this: forgetting what is behind me, and reaching out for that which lies ahead, I press towards the goal to win the prize which is God's call in the life above in Christ Jesus" (Phil. 3:13,14). That's the summons to adventure—and it's in the Bible.

Speak to us, O God, in our confusion and our groping. Use the words of Holy Scripture to anchor our faith in thee and to launch us out to discover new truth and act on it with alacrity and joy. Give us the open mind and receptive heart to which thy Word can speak through Jesus Christ our Lord. Amen.

5

When I Stopped Explaining Human Suffering

"I can explain all the poems that ever were invented," said Humpty Dumpty, "and a good many that haven't been invented just yet." Lewis Carroll, the author of *Alice in Wonderland*, had his own delightful way of satirizing the modern world. We recognize Humpty Dumpty here as the "Great Explainer." From infancy we've all been subjected to him. In answer to our childhood questions, we've been bombarded with explanations of everything from the ticking of a clock to the solar system, and we've grown up to believe that there must be an explanation for everything. Yet, every now and then doubt creeps in, and it is getting stronger as we move toward the end of this century. Can everything be explained? Must everything be explained? It's dawning on us that there are limits to the activities of the "Great Explainer." When Humpty Dumpty claims to be able to explain all the poems that were ever invented, we realize that this is exactly what we don't need. It is almost a definition of a great poem that it cannot be explained, and most of us remember the absurdity of those schoolboy exercises in which we were required to turn great poetry into flat, explanatory prose. Perhaps we are now more willing to admit that there are areas of life—indeed, the most important areas—where explanations are out of place. The rediscovery of mystery may be one of the great adventures of this generation.

Alice, in another encounter, makes the point with beautiful precision. "Explain yourself," said the Caterpillar. "I can't explain *myself*, I'm afraid, sir," said Alice. Neither can you or I. The mystery of our existence—why I am I, and you are you, and what we are supposed to be doing on earth—are not things to be explained like the workings of a clock. The self is a mystery; the soul is a mystery; love is a mystery; and so, supremely, is God.

Why, then, have preachers joined the company of the "Great Explainers"? In my own ministry I have to confess that a great deal of my time has been spent offering explanations of religion. I've tried to explain what the Bible means, what the Christian Gospel really is, what prayer can be expected to do, what kind of society the Church is, why we believe in eternal life, and a hundred other things. Now I'm not saying that I've come to believe that all this was a waste of time. It's no more a waste of time to employ our minds in understanding the claims of religion than it is to seek explanations of any other human activity or facet of the universe. When I said that there are mysteries that we accept rather than explain I didn't mean that we should cease to seek answers wherever we can. A great poem or piece of music is ultimately a mystery, but that doesn't mean that literary or musical studies and interpretations are valueless. The soul is ultimately a mystery, but that recognition doesn't rule out all the researches of psychology. God is the supreme mystery, but that is not an excuse for abandoning all efforts to understand him, or all explanations of the teachings of the great religions. In fact, we are commanded to love him "with all our mind." So anyone has the right to ask a believer to explain what his faith means to him, and that is really what I am doing in this series of talks. We should beware of the person who shouts, "Mystery," when asked to explain some apparently irrational belief.

No, I don't regret or renounce attempts to explain Christian faith insofar as they may help to clarify claims that are made and clear up misconceptions. But I have become more and more aware of the limits of explanation. In the New Testament we are told to be "prepared to make a defense to any one who calls you to account for the hope that is in you" (I Pet. 3:15). But I remember that Paul, who was an expert at such defense and explanation, spoke of the resurrection, declaring: "Behold, I show you a mystery" (I Cor. 15:51). Without the element of mystery there is no religion, no real faith. How many people have been argued into the kingdom of God? Explanations may serve to pull down some of the barriers of misunderstanding that keep modern men and women from commitment to Christ, but in the end faith responds to a mystery that appeals to the depths beyond the mind.

All this is by way of explaining why there are times when I stop explaining. One such time, without question, is when I am asked concerning some terrible experience of human suffering. "Why did this happen if God is love?" I left the seminary full of explanations of the problem of suffering. I knew the argument that suffering is the inevitable result of our free will: God took the risk of things going wrong, and we're better off being free and having to endure suffering than being spared all pain and having no choice. I knew the argument that talks of the educative value of suffering and points to the achievement of the saints who used their pain to bring them nearer to God. I knew the metaphor of the tapestry: we see all the tangled threads on the wrong side; only God sees the real picture, but one day we too shall see how even the most terrible things are woven into his great design.

I haven't thrown away these arguments. I believe there is truth in all of them. But for a long time now I have ceased to offer them as explanations to anyone who is crushed by suffering. They are the kind of thoughts that may indeed suggest to us in a time of calm reflection and discussion how pain may be understood in the fabric of human life. But I have discovered that they are not what I want either to hear or to offer in moments of real anguish. You might say that I stopped explaining suffering when faced with real events whose horror numbs the mind and ties the tongue.

Every day there are fearful tragedies enacted that defy any real explanation. If we stop to think about the earthquakes, the wars, the kidnappings, and the murders we hear about every day from the media, the full weight of the problem of human suffering must appall us. But somehow we are so made that the problem never seems acute until it comes close to us. Then we cry out to God with the psalmist: "Why dost thou hide thy face, heedless of our misery and sufferings?" (Ps. 44:24). When I hear someone say, "Since that terrible thing happened I haven't been able to believe in God," I understand, but can't help wondering why we don't think this way about the other terrible things that have happened and are happening to other people since the beginnings of the human race. The statistics of tragedy are overwhelming, but one single event is enough to make us ask, "My God, why?"

Let me tell you about Roger. All of us have stories from our own experience, distant or recent, that raise this agonizing question. I have chosen this one because it happened many years ago—at about the time, in fact, that I had given up explaining human suffering. Roger was a young Scottish army officer in World War II, who was not a professional soldier but a chemist by profession. He and I were in the same outfit, and we were both taken prisoner during the campaign in France in 1940. He had been married a few months at this time, and his wife was expecting a baby. In the prison camps we were in together, Roger was one of the quiet, cheerful ones, openhearted and generous when being generous was not easy. He was thoughtful too about his religion, which was very real and quite unostentatious. In such trying times Roger was the kind of unassuming, humorous, and steady lad you like to have around. In due time Roger heard of the birth of his child, and we all rejoiced with him.

Then, as the years went by, he watched this child he had never seen grow up in the photographs that came from home: one, two, three, four years old. Finally the time came when he could expect to celebrate his child's fifth birthday at home. The Allied armies were racing toward our camp in the spring of 1945. It was a time of great confusion, as our captors sought to move prisoners from the path of the advancing liberators. Roger's camp was ordered out, and a trail of prisoners took to the roads under escort. Then one day an Allied plane swooped out of the skies and, not recognizing the prisoners, loosed a blast of machine-gun fire. Roger was killed.

There was no way for a chaplain, or anyone else, to explain that. It's only one of thousands of such tragedies that war and accident bring. But is it explanation we really seek at such a time? Isn't it much more an ability to absorb the tragedy, to seek and respond to the God who has not promised explanations but grace to endure? At such a time one doesn't need answers to questions so much as a strength from within. That doesn't mean just quiet accept-ance. Why should we stifle our protests? Job didn't; nor did the psalmists. Neither did Jesus in the Garden of Gethsema-ne or in his cry from the cross. What matters is how we come through.

I believe the Christian Gospel not because it offers the best explanation of human suffering, but because it gives us the strength we need to win through. The name Jesus, after all, does not mean "Explainer" but "Savior," and at such a time it is a Savior, a deliverer, that we need. The story of his passion, the way in which this man of purity and love was hounded to his death, says more to me than any argu-ments about why such suffering is allowed in God's uni-verse. For, if innocent suffering is what appalls us, here is at once the greatest imaginable suffering and the greatest innocence. And yet here the Bible tells us, "God was in

Christ reconciling the world unto himself" (2 Cor. 5:19). So the God I trust knows all about suffering, and is neither indifferent nor detached. He let his Son go through the worst any one of us can experience, and there is no hell that he has not known and from which he cannot rescue us. To me Jesus is alive. His Resurrection was not just a three-day wonder. It was God's answer to the cross, and is his answer to the cross we must bear. He has given us a Savior who, as the New Testament says, "was made perfect through suffering." He can see us through.

Even if a time comes when all this fails to inspire our faith—when the stress of mental and physical pain makes our deepest convictions seem to fade—we can still ask ourselves what the options are. Under the weight of a shattering blow we can, of course, stay with our protest and let a mood of anger and bitterness sour our lives forever. "Curse God and die" was at first all that Job's wife had to offer him in the way of sympathy. To decide on a life based on such a response to tragedy is to condemn oneself indeed to a living death. Would we really want to go that way, shriveling up inside, soured in mind and heart?

The other possibility is what you might call the stoic one. There are those who refuse to give way to bitterness, or to curse their God, but simply shrug their shoulders and steel themselves for the grim road ahead. I have known, and admired, men and women who went the stoic way of sheer acceptance. "This is life," they seem to say. "That's how it is and there's no use fussing and fretting." Yes, the Stoic has courage, like Shakespeare's Brutus of whom it was said: "This was the noblest Roman of them all. /His life was gentle and the elements/ So mixed in him that Nature might stand up/ And say to all the world, 'This was a man.'"

Let me tell you why I could not be satisfied with the stoic response. It is not bitter; yet, when we shrug our shoulders and carry on, something inside dies. First, one loses contact with a living, vibrant God of love and settles for a fatalism in the soul. Not only pain but joy is then

robbed of that enriching grace that could be called the
"sympathy of God." Second, the stoic is bound to lose the
quality of compassion with another's sorrow. If I succeed in
this dogged acceptance of calamity, I must expect others to
do the same. Stoicism is a kind of aristocratic virtue that
despises the weaknesses of the common man or woman.
There was no such stoicism in Jesus.

What other response to tragedy is there than that of
bitterness, stoicism, or what I call the Christian way? Do
you understand why I call it the "way" and not the "explanation"? Arguments fall silent when we are in darkness, but
I believe that there is always a light to show us the way.
When I glimpse this light, and stumble toward the way, I
realize that I am not alone. What greater encouragement is
there at such times than what the creed calls "the communion of the saints." I know that I am surrounded by men
and women whom I have admired and loved, who went
through suffering trusting boldly in God. From biblical
times to the present day they witnessed to me, and what
they say drowns out the bitter words of the defeated and
the brave words of the stoic. They don't offer me their
explanations but the testimony of their lives. And they
remind me of the Savior who saw them through to victory.

It's easy to rattle off the words from the King James
Bible: "All things work together for good to them that love
God" (Rom. 8:28), but we are entitled to protest that things
do not always work together for good, even for the most
loving. It was a relief to me to know that Paul didn't say
that. He said: "We know that in everything God works for
good with those who love him." That, to me, means more
than any theory about why we suffer. "In everything," yes,
in everything, no matter how awful, God can work with us
for good if we love him. And how can we not love him if
we know what kind of a Savior he has given us, "who was
acquainted with grief . . . stricken, smitten of God, and afflicted . . . and with whose stripes we are healed" (Isa.
53:3,4,5).

We confess, O God, that there is much we have to suffer that we do not understand, and that we are sometimes overwhelmed by the cruelty and injustice of our world. Remind us of thy love in Christ, and strengthen us to believe that thou canst work in all things for good through the power of his cross. Amen.

6

My Conscience—Right or Wrong

Whatever the word God means for most of us today, I suspect it's tied very closely to what we call *conscience*. Even those who do not practice any formal kind of worship and would have difficulty in expressing their religious beliefs would admit that they are subject to the promptings— and sometimes the naggings—of an inner voice that speaks about right and wrong. And they would have little difficulty in identifying this as the voice of God. When I try to think back to my earliest religious experiences, the word *God* certainly carries with it memories of conscience, good and bad. If I described how faith works in my life today, I'd have to reckon with this inner voice that seems to approve or disapprove, to encourage or rebuke.

One of the by-products of our recent political history has been a new national awareness of the question of conscience. The word seemed suddenly to be on everyone's lips. We heard people asking how men in positions of high responsibility could indulge in deceit and "dirty tricks" with a good conscience. The word *unconscionable* was tossed around—a resounding adjective that literally means "not according to conscience." As a procession of witnesses flickered across our television screens during the Watergate hearings, we found ourselves asking: "Guilty or not guilty, is this a person of conscience, with some sensitivity to matters of right and wrong?" After some years of relative indifference to matters of private and public morality the question jumped to the forefront of our national thinking. We realized that, while we don't expect our statesmen and their associates to be paragons of virtue and wisdom, we do expect them to have a decent conscience in working order.

More important than our judgment on those in public office has been the awakening of the conscience of the average citizen. All sensitive persons have had to think again about the little ways in which we have learned to still the voice of conscience. When we have watched others paraded before us with their transgressions exposed we must surely have wondered at times: "How would I stand up to such a searchlight on my soul?" A significant result of the tragic Watergate affair was the realization that all of us had a share in this blunting of conscience, and that we need a revival of our own ethical sensitivity. A little story I read somewhere illustrates what I mean. A lady driving her car out of a parking lot scraped some paint from a new vehicle parked alongside. As there were no witnesses around she was about to drive away. "Then," she said, "I remembered Watergate and went back to write a little note leaving my name and address."

Religion, I believe, has a lot to do with conscience, and the Church has been said to be the conscience of the nation. But the Church is not an official institution to which we can hand over the task of keeping society on a straight path. It may have been like that in the Middle Ages. It wasn't in New Testament times, when Christians were a tiny minority with little public influence. And it certainly isn't like that today. The Church consists of people like you and me. If the Church has failed in this matter, then we have failed. If the Church is to challenge the nation's conscience, it is our conscience that is being challenged. The power of the Church to raise moral standards and cleanse public life resides simply in the practice and persuasion of its members.

How then should religion be active in order to keep the conscience in working order? For some a simple answer suffices. The Bible, they would say, tells us about right and wrong and the believer merely has to follow his conscience in choosing one and avoiding the other. All of us heard as children about that little inner voice. We've got to obey it. That's the voice of God and that's the answer to the whole question. What more need be said? Among the other things we discover if we listen to the Bible and reflect on our own experience is that listening to this inner voice doesn't resolve all questions about our behavior. And the Bible, in fact, doesn't picture the moral life as a series of clear choices between right and wrong in which we are infallibly guided by our conscience. The Bible has a lot more to say about the conscience than just the advice to obey it at all costs. We learn that there is no guarantee that when we follow our conscience we shall infallibly do what is right. You and I may each act conscientiously and yet come to diametrically opposite conclusions as to what we ought to do.

We have had numerous examples in the 1970s of people of conscience reaching opposite conclusions. The question of amnesty, whether applied to former President Nixon or to draft-evaders and deserters quite clearly divides men and women of sincere conscience. What one feels to be his conscientious conviction may be flatly contradicted by the conscience of someone else. We cannot accuse all those who differ from us of being "unconscionable." The still, small voice is obviously not saying exactly the same thing to everyone who tries to listen.

Unfortunately, history is crowded with examples, not only of mistakes, but of heinous cruelties and persecutions wrought by people who believed they were following their conscience. The Apostle Paul would readily confess that he was obeying his conscience when, as Saul of Tarsus, he encouraged stoning the martyr Stephen and dragged Christians off to prison. He felt he was being "zealous toward God." Most of the inquisitors were acting according to their conscience in delivering their victims to be tortured. John Calvin certainly acted conscientiously in allowing Servetus to be burned. Clearly the Christian way cannot be simply described as following one's conscience. A living religion must mean something more than just listening to the inner voice.

The word *conscience* is a comparative newcomer to the human vocabulary. It arose when the philosophers of ancient Greece began to distinguish between moral rules that were imposed from without, and our inner assent to them. The word literally indicates a second way of knowing. If I am confronted by a demand by the state or public opinion to take a certain course of action, I know that this is required of me. But at the same time I have a second kind of knowledge—the knowledge that there is a voice within me that may resist this demand. Every advance in human ethical sensitivity has been brought about by those, like the prophets of Israel, who rejected the current moral rules of their day in the name of this inner voice. In the Christian view, the word *conscience* came to mean the conviction that the will of God revealed in Christ is our ultimate authority and that when God speaks through the inner voice we have no choice but to obey. No other authority can take its place.

Christianity thus became, in spite of many lapses, the great upholder of the rights of conscience, and the Church has gradually worked its way toward a complete respect for the conscience of individuals, whether or not they accept the Christian faith. The Bible honors those who heed the inner directions of the heart. The Old Testament doesn't use the word *conscience* but when we read of David, for instance, that "his heart smote him," we know what was at work. Although Jesus didn't speak about conscience, we see from the Gospels how his very presence acted to stimulate the sleepy consciences of all kinds of people, from those who wanted to stone the woman taken in adultery to the stony hearts of Herod and Pilate. The Bible views conscience as the channel for knowing and obeying the will of God. Therefore, it is to be obeyed, exalted, and respected. But our conscience is not God. We remain sinners whose consciences can be corrupted like any other part of us. It is only when we lose sight of the ultimate sovereignty of God and our own sinfulness that we can make an idol of conscience and develop the arrogance of the self-righteous and the myth of our own infallibility. Religious people need to listen to the advice given by Oliver Cromwell to my Scottish ancestors: "I beseech you, brethren, in the bowels of Christ, conceive it possible you may be mistaken."

For me, living religion means honoring the conscience, but at the same time realizing that my conscience may become dulled, seared, or distorted. At the same time, I recognize that one's conscience can be educated, sensitized, and made to conform with the mind of Christ. Let me sum up what I believe the Bible tells us about conscience.

1. It means keeping alive that inner voice in spite of the enormous pressures on us to conform to the standards of the world around us. Is there one of us who cannot think of some point at which our conscience is not as sensitive as it used to be? It could be strict truthfulness, concern for the hungry and the oppressed, self-indulgence, control of the tongue, or willingness to take a stand for what we believe. To keep the conscience clear means renewing the vows of loyalty to Christ that lead a man or woman to say like Luther, "Here stand I. I can do no other. So help me God."

2. At the same time, the fact that we must keep a clear conscience is a continual reminder that conscience is not infallible. We must therefore have utmost respect for the conscience of others. Paul, in a moving passage, deals with a question of conscience that has arisen in the Corinthian church. There were some whose conscience forbade them to eat meat that had been offered to idols. Paul thinks they were wrong. His conscience had risen above such petty

taboos. But he tells his followers to respect the conscience of such "weaker brothers" and to do nothing to offend them. A Christian Church should be a place where fallibility is admitted and where sensitive people learn to accept their differences in the spirit of Christ.

3. By such Scriptures we are reminded, too, that educating the conscience is not merely a matter of making it more sensitive. Some of the early Christians obviously needed to be less sensitive in certain areas that Paul considered unimportant. Keeping a clear conscience may well mean purging our inner life of things that were once imposed on us as part of our Christian obedience. Jesus used to speak of people who had tremendous conscience about certain religious practices, such as weighing out strict tenths of every herb on their shelves, but were totally insensitive to obvious injustice round the corner. It is possible for a Christian today to suffer ancestral twinges of conscience about playing golf on Sunday and care little about the great moral issues of our day.

Above all, keeping a clear conscience must mean constantly turning to Christ. He is the great educator of the human conscience. To live with him is to absorb his standards and be sensitized by his spirit. By exposing ourselves to Christian worship, by studying the Bible, by the communion of prayer, and by sharing with others our aspirations, failures, and hopes we learn the mind of Christ, and train our conscience to respond to the inner voice without arrogance or self-deception. And Christ meets the greatest need of every one of us who seeks to live by the light of conscience. He offers forgiveness for our sins. This is the good news—that we may rejoice in the words: "Go in peace: thy sins are forgiven." This is the difference the Gospel makes to the man or woman of conscience. Without forgiveness there is no end to the agony of a bad conscience. God gives us in Christ the clearing of our conscience, freeing us from that nagging that "makes cowards of us all" and makes the call to follow him not a duty but a joy.

"*Almighty and everlasting God, who art always more ready to hear than we to pray, and art wont to give more than either we desire or deserve; pour down upon us the abundance of thy mercy; forgiving us those things whereof our conscience is afraid, and giving us those good things which we are not worthy to ask, but through the merits and mediation of Jesus Christ, thy Son, our Lord. Amen.*" (Collect from the *Book of Common Prayer*)

7

Thoughts When I Conduct a Funeral

There are two occasions which draw almost everyone in this country to church from time to time—weddings and funerals. Even those who never attend Sunday services of worship show up because of their affection for the bride or bridegroom or respect for the deceased. As a minister conducting such services, I sometimes find myself wondering how much they mean to those unfamiliar with religious ceremonies and religious language, and what passes through their minds as they listen. Then it occurred to me that, conversely, such people must often be asking what the service means to the one who is conducting it. What is he actually thinking about as he speaks the conventional words and goes through the motions associated with a wedding or a funeral?

Though I'm going to try to answer that question from my own point of view, I imagine that my thoughts at such a time are not very different from those of my colleagues in the ministry. By speaking frankly about my thoughts when conducting a funeral or memorial service, I hope to share with you what I have come to believe about sorrow, bereavement, and death in light of the Christian Gospel.

Some people may be surprised to learn that a minister

has any particular thoughts at all at such a time unless the deceased is a close friend or relative. I find that there's a common tendency to believe that in such instances a minister or priest is simply doing a professional job. Many assume he's trained to say and do the right things and can't be expected to involve himself personally in what is going on. Anyone who has ever heard a wedding or a funeral service gabbled off in a mechanical way, as if someone has just pressed the right button, could be excused for getting this impression. But any minister who is truly a pastor and has human sensitivities could never officiate on such occasions without giving thought to the meaning of what he is doing and saying or about the people gathered there before him.

Since, however, any action or form of words can lose its power by dint of constant repetition—and in the course of a long ministry a clergyman could conduct well over a thousand funerals—I remind myself every time, as I do at a wedding, that for those most deeply concerned, this is a unique occasion. For them it has supreme importance, and therefore one has no right to view this service as just one among many. I believe that we are engaged in giving thanks for one, unique and precious life, and commending to God one of his children whom he values as an individual human being. There can be no question of just rattling off a standard form of words as though one funeral were just the same as any other. This came home to me with special force when, as an army chaplain, I sometimes had the sad duty of conducting funeral services in circumstances of danger and need for haste. Even there, I tried to concentrate on each individual, realizing what he meant to those who would soon hear the news of his death.

That leads me to speak of the presence at most funerals of those who have been bereaved of a close relative or very dear friend. The minister must think of them, entering in some way into their sorrow and sense of loss. I may or may not know them well, but I nearly always try to talk with them about the service. Whatever their response to the shock of what has happened to them—and there is always some shock, even if the death was long expected and even welcomed as a release—I hope to turn their thoughts to the promise of God and the Christian hope of a life beyond. At such times we all need to be reminded that the Bible does not minimize the reality of death, and therefore the Church should avoid pathetic attempts to prolong the appearance of life or to focus attention on the mortal remains and their resting-place. There should be no pretense about a Christian funeral. We die, says the Bible, and our hope is focused on the God, who tells us of a resurrection life and promises that he will work for good in all things with those who love him.

So, as I look at the mourners, I pray that the words of Scripture and the prayers will turn their thoughts to the resources of the Gospel, the good news of eternal life in Jesus Christ our Lord. Genuine sympathy must be there, and sympathy means "feeling with." At times this "feeling with" on the part of the minister is so powerful, because of his closeness to the family or the tragedy of the occasion, that it is hard to keep control; at other times he may be much less involved. What matters is that the promises of God should be proclaimed and Christian belief affirmed. What the bereaved are looking for is not just someone to share their sorrow but a rock to cling to. I try to remember that. This is why, although I respond to requests to include certain readings, prayers, or music, provided they are in tune with the Christian faith, I would never be persuaded to redesign the service in such a way as to mute the great assurances of the Gospel. Real sympathy is more than a sentiment: it means offering the only faith that sustains.

One of the difficulties of a funeral service is striking a balance between the traditional declaration of the Church's faith and a personal remembrance of the one who has died. A totally impersonal service is cold and formal, leaving the mourners to their own thoughts and memories. Yet a service that focuses entirely on the person being remembered and committed to God tends to be a sentimental farewell in which the note of the Gospel is drowned out by eulogies, memories, and tears. The practice in my own church is to use the form of service in our book of order, to select among the Scriptures those most appropriate for the occasion, and to include a commemorative prayer in which thanks are given for the unique qualities of life and service in the one we are commending to God.

What, then, am I apt to be thinking about when our thoughts turn to the one who has died? If I knew the person well, I should, of course, share the mixture of sad and happy thoughts that abound at such a time. But, whoever it is, I do not fix my attention on the body. I don't think of the deceased as sleeping in a coffin, but as alive in the world eternal. This is something not easy to express. I don't mean that I ignore the earthly remains or reject the impulse to honor and respect them. It's just that I believe the real person is now in another dimension. Jesus told us that God is not the God of the dead but of the living, adding that "all live unto him." He clearly believed that to have God as our Father now is to have him as such forever. So when my thoughts turn to the one whose funeral it is, for me that person is no longer there where the body lies, but in the eternal presence. Here I must add something quite personal which is not based on any particular Scripture or belief of the Church. I find that some people seem especially real and near during their own funeral service. And these are the ones who give me the impression of being near to God during their mortal life—the kind of people we sometimes call saints. It is they who contribute to the special joy that can attend the last rites of those who have fought the good fight and kept the faith and finished the course.

So conducting a funeral service is neither a routine nor necessarily a mournful business. I have known few more inspiring moments in worship than when a saint of God is commemorated and committed to him with the triumphant hallelujahs of his Church on earth. The Apostle Paul told his flock not to grieve "as those who have no hope." Our grief is real, but so is the comfort in Christ. Jesus' grief was real when a friend died, as he was on his way to Jerusalem for the last time. The shortest verse in the Bible tells us that when he was told that Lazarus was dead, "Jesus wept." But the miracle of Lazarus being raised is a symbol of the power of Jesus over death and all its sorrow. "Death is swallowed up in victory" are the words that should dominate a Christian funeral, for, like Paul, "I am persuaded that neither death, nor life, nor angels, nor principalities, nor powers, nor things present, nor things to come, nor height, nor depth, nor any other creature, shall be able to separate us from the love of God, which is in Christ Jesus our Lord" (Rom. 8:38,39). I repeat these words at every funeral service, and every time I hear them afresh as the Word of God on which I base my hope.

But now I must face a very different question. Granted, it can be a joy to pay tribute to a good man or woman whom you know to have lived and died in communion with God. But how do you feel when the deceased is a very different kind of person—one either you didn't know or who was not so loved and respected, or who made it clear that the Church and its faith meant little to him? Is there not some hypocrisy in proclaiming the great promises and speaking about virtues they may not have possessed? There certainly would be hypocrisy if we spoke as if a certain notorious sinner were really one of the saints and implied that a self-centered and spiteful person need only die in order to enter into eternal joy. But there is no hypocrisy in announcing the Gospel as it comes through the words at such a service. It remains true no matter what one person's response to it may have been. And there is no hypocrisy in giving thanks for any life that has evoked even a minimum of love and gratitude. Is there anyone so bereft of any good gift that no one felt even a moment's pang on his passing?

We must remember that here, of all times and places, the words of Jesus strike deep: "Judge not." As a minister it is not my task to assess the worth of every life completed on earth and thus commended to our God. I can affirm without hesitation that any life clearly turned toward God will pass on to live and grow in his presence. About a life that showed little concern for God or neighbor, I can pass no judgment, for only God knows all the circumstances and the inner motives of the heart. So I commend them to his mercy, believing, as I do, in his infinite grace and compassion. It was Robert Burns who wrote:

> Who made the heart, 'tis he alone
> Decidedly can try us;
> He knows each chord, its various tone,
> Each spring its various bias.

He went on to remind us of how little we know of each other's temptations:

> What's done we partly may compute,
> But know not what's resisted.

This same sense of ignorance and frailty comes over me when I find myself conducting a service after a particularly tragic or unexpected death. I cannot avoid mentioning the funeral of a child snatched away by a grim disease, a youth killed in a moment by a drunken driver, a mother taken from her young children by a malignancy, or a suicide. What does one feel, and what can one say? Again, the sympathy must overflow, but not to the extent that the minister himself is unable to offer comfort and hope. We must honestly acknowledge that there is no easy answer to such tragedies. But again the conviction must shine through that the God who knows in his Son the agony of the cross is able to lift us to a place where sorrow is transcended and life renewed. Here too my belief in the eternal dimension gives me assurance that within God's love nothing is ever lost, nothing is forever wasted. I believe that there will be fulfilment in another sphere for all whose time seems to have been tragically cut off.

Though this may seem a strange approach to the subjects of eternal life and remembrance, I've taken it because I'm speaking about the faith here in quite personal terms. That leads me to one final thought. As one gets older, the thought is bound to cross one's mind that "someday *I'll* be the one for whom a service like this will be conducted." You may have this thought on the occasion of a funeral. We should not be obsessed with it, but there's nothing morbid about an occasional reminder of our own mortality; it's the strongest test of all we really believe. I pray that in the end our own hope will be in the mercy of God and the promises of the Gospel. I like then to remember the first question and answer of an historical document of the faith, the Heidelberg Catechism. "What is your only comfort, in life and in death?" "That I belong—body and soul, in life and in death—not to myself but to my faithful Savior, Jesus Christ."

O God, who has committed unto us the swift and solemn trust of life, grant that we may so live in faith and hope and love that we may be ready for entrance into the eternal world where we shall find, with all thy children the fulfillment of thy plan; through Jesus Christ our Lord. Amen.

8

"I'm Praying for You"
—So What?

People who have listened to my sermons on radio often
write: "Please pray for me." When I answer them, it's natural to conclude by saying: "I'm praying for you." One day
not long ago I began to think about this. I felt there was a
danger of using this expression too casually, as if it were
something expected of a minister at any time. So I decided
that in the future I would not write these words without
pausing then and there to offer the prayer I was promising.
Then I began to ask myself some questions about such
prayers that I want to share with you.

I began with the question, "Just what am I expecting
from this prayer, especially for someone I did not know and
whose circumstances it was difficult to picture?" Would
something really happen because in a moment of quiet I
offered this name to God for blessing? It occurred to me
that many in our skeptical world would respond to the
statement, "I'm praying for you," with "So what?" For those
of us raised in the Christian tradition this kind of response
is disconcerting. We have been taught to assume that it's
good to have someone praying for us, and that we ought to
be constantly praying for others. Yet perhaps there are

times when deep down there is a little whisper of "I wonder what good it really does?"

I began to think about what the Bible says about prayer. At first I thought about the complaints that are recorded
there so bluntly, by the psalmists, Job, and some of the
prophets that God did not listen to their prayers. Evidently
we are not the first generation to experience doubts about
the efficacy of prayer. But I realized that these occasional
complaints were uttered in the context of a general and
often fervent belief that prayer is not only helpful but a
necessity, and that it has a real effect on people's lives. The
Bible tells us about those who were too proud to pray, too
self-satisfied to pray, or too unbelieving to pray. But its great
characters are men and women who prayed for others
without reserve or embarrassment, and felt a tremendous
compulsion to do so.

The prophetic figures in the Bible, great national leaders like Abraham, Moses, Samuel, Elijah, or Isaiah, and the
apostolic leaders like Peter and Paul, were as varied in
character and temperament as any representative group of
twentieth-century statesmen or church leaders—and they
were as deeply involved in the politics of their day. Almost
every situation known to us, from the most heroic to the
most scandalous, can be paralleled in the pages of the
Bible, and these men played their parts in them as skillfully
or clumsily as their modern counterparts. They were not
gurus sitting on mountaintops or in caves, issuing words of
wisdom, but men of action. And they had one peculiar
characteristic that is bound to strike us today: they prayed
for their people. I'm not implying that modern leaders never pray, but to these Bible characters prayer was foremost in
their thoughts. They saw themselves as intercessors before
all else. They wrestled with God on behalf of their nation,
their community, and their friends and enemies—often
with passion, indignation, or even anger.

It may be difficult for us to understand how deeply
they felt about praying for others. Moses, you remember,

was often driven to distraction by the Israelites he was leading through the desert, and was tempted to wash his hands of them and go his own way. Yet back he came to the Lord to plead for them. Once when he came down from Sinai with the oracles of God and found that in his absence the people had thrown an orgy around the golden idols they had made, he lost his temper, and there was bloodshed in the camp. But then he turned again to prayer: "Oh, this people have sinned a great sin, and have made them gods of gold. Yet now, if thou wilt forgive their sin—; and if not, blot me, I pray thee, out of thy book" (Exod. 32:31,32). What a passionate, Christlike prayer that was, and how different from our perfunctory prayers for the peace of the world, or the welfare of the nation.

One of the most striking words I know about intercessory prayers comes from the lips of the Prophet Samuel. At the time, he was thoroughly out of tune with his people, and disgusted by their desire for a king. He warned them in no uncertain terms of all the disasters that would follow if the nation forgot the sovereign Lord who had created and redeemed them. Yet he felt bound to continue his intercessions for them. "God forbid," he said, "that I should sin against the Lord in ceasing to pray for you." I can hardly imagine anyone listening to him being tempted to say, "So what?"

This wasn't a formal acknowledgment like some of the official prayers of our day. It wasn't just a routine, "God bless the people." It was surely the expression of Samuel's belief that we are meant to pray for one another, that this is a vital part of our faith, and that not to do so is to sin. Samuel was making his farewell as a national leader, but from one obligation he could not retire. One duty was laid on him so long as he had breath in his body. He would continue to perform the greatest task God had laid upon him. "God forbid that I should sin against the Lord in ceasing to pray for you" (1 Sam. 12:23).

Do you and I feel as strongly as this about the prayers we make for other people, either in our homes, or in church? Are our intercessions so important to us that we would think it a sin to leave them out? Can we honestly say that intercession—praying for others—is a major factor in our daily lives, something it would be a sin to neglect?

It's often said that we live in such a different world from the people of the Bible that we can't have the same kind of belief. We assume they found it much easier to think of God intervening as a result of prayer. Perhaps. Many today find it almost impossible to believe that anything really happens when we ask God to do something for us, let alone for other people. It's assumed that intercession is really an outpouring of our longings for someone's welfare, and is thus a kind of therapeutic exercise for our own souls. In formal worship, intercession may be viewed as a simple expression of our hopes for the nation and the world. We do live in a different world than that of biblical times, and I don't want to construct an elaborate argument for prayer today. I simply want to confront the fact that the world of the Bible where prayers are made and heard is the world that Jesus accepted, and at the deepest level you and I are still in the same world today. Nothing has been discovered that rubs out of human experience the mystery of communion with God, and the unfathomable ways in which our lives are linked together for good and evil within the human family. We can seal ourselves off from this dimension if we like, and live as though there were no mystery of interdependence—as though human lives are so much data fed into the cosmic computer with totally predictable results. But real living begins now, as it did then, with recognition of the mystery and the acceptance of a world where God, our neighbors, you, and I are somehow linked together.

The trend is not necessarily away from belief in intercessory prayer. I receive more requests now for special prayers than I did many years ago. There is a great residual belief in intercession in this land of ours. This is why I am taking up the question of its real value.

"I'm praying for you." "So what?" The answer, of

course, depends a good deal on the spirit in which the
promise of prayer is given, even the tone of voice. Think of
the different ways in which we can say, "I am praying for
you." It can mean nothing more than an expression of
sympathy, assuring someone of our good will. But if we
don't really mean to pray we should find something else to
say. Again, it can be said with a genuine mental resolve to
ask God's blessing on that person when next we pray, perhaps to put the name down in some little book we use for
intercessions. Unfortunately, it can also be said with a kind
of barb, implying that the other person needs conversion to
a better frame of mind. Can you imagine anything more
infuriating than someone with whom you are having a
tremendous row suddenly smiling sweetly and saying: "I am
praying for you"? But thank God there are people from
whom we can hear these words with immense comfort and
joy. They are the ones who don't use the phrase glibly, or
as a conventional expression of goodwill. Nor do they give
the impression that it's all a matter of course. Still less do
they imply that there's something about us they hope to
change. There is, in fact, a kind of person to whose promise
of prayer few would want to reply, "So what?"

The value of the words "I'm praying for you" really
depends on the sincerity and saintliness of the one who
makes this remark. Most of us are short on saintliness but
sincerity is within our reach. Sincerity depends a great deal
on our conviction that when we pray something happens.
Let me say right away that I believe something happens. It
is inconceivable to me that prayer does no more than re-
lieve our minds or express our sympathy.

I think of that fast-moving first chapter in Mark's Gospel. There we find Jesus overwhelmed by the needs of
ordinary people, both friends and strangers. All day he
pours himself out in teaching and healing, sensitive to the
tremendous needs of body and soul around him. Then he
goes to the synagogue to pray and preach. He returns at
nightfall, thoroughly weary, to the house where Peter and
Andrew live, and, instead of having a rest, he is greeted by

the news that Peter's mother-in-law has a fever and needs his help. Finally, with darkness falling, and looking forward to a long sleep, Jesus finds the house surrounded by hundreds of the sick and disturbed. Do we then read that he retired to bed and planned a day off? "In the morning," wrote Mark, "rising up a great while before day, he went out, and departed into a solitary place, and there prayed" (Mark 1:35). For Christ, it was not a case of being too busy to pray, but of being too busy not to pray. He was surely praying for all those people he had met and those he was going to meet. He would pray too for his disciples that they too might have his healing gifts. Do you believe that if he had returned that morning and said, as he did on another occasion, "I am praying for you" that any one of them would have said, "So what?"

I have no idea how intercession works. That's probably one of our foolish modern questions. Do we ask how love works? God doesn't always immediately give us the good things we request for someone else. Yet I find it impossible to believe that God is unwilling to act until a certain number of people have mentioned a particular person's name in their prayers. I also know that our lives are much more closely linked than we realize, and that just as prayer is my own link with God, it can also be the way in which we are linked through him to others. Sometimes we think of prayer as a direct line between us and God. Perhaps we should think of prayer as a kind of triangle—God, you, and the one you are praying for. That is a richer concept. Still richer is the one where we realize that our intercessions are opening the whole human drama to the inflowing of God's grace. That is what happens when, alone or in a church, we pray for such things as the moral renewal of our nation, and justice and peace in the world. We are accepting our part in the human drama with its joys and sorrows, its peace and violence, its health and sickness, and making an opening through which God's healing grace can flow, so the heavenly will be better done on earth. To pray for a special person is to open a channel for the entrance of this grace.

The more we enter into the mind of Christ, the more meaning have the words "I am praying for you," and the more we begin to understand what intercession really is. For then we shall be delivered from the delusion that to pray for others means asking God to make them the kind of person we think they should be. This is one of the besetting sins of religious people. Sincere prayer for someone means asking God to do what he knows is best for them. And wouldn't you want that prayer?

In the presence of Christ I know that I must keep praying for all sorts of people—those very close to me and those about whom I know little. God knows about all of them and loves to hear us pray for them. The New Testament pictures Jesus as the supreme intercessor—the one who pleaded for the whole human family and yet could say to a single wavering disciple, "I have prayed for thee, that thy faith fail not" (Luke 22:32). Jesus is still praying for us. He is praying in us. And he is praying through us for the men and women he has redeemed. It is he who gives new life and meaning to the simple words "I am praying for you."

Father God, we pray today for one another, all who have been listening and thinking at this time, alone or in families. Give thy grace to each one as thou seest the need, and keep us constant and believing as we daily remember others in our prayers; through the power of him who, even now, is praying for us, Jesus Christ, thy Son. Amen.

9

When Love Gets Tired

There is an awkward moment in every preacher's experience. He has just delivered a sermon on Christian love, spelling out its obligations, stressing its practicality and its application to every human being no matter how depraved or unlovable. Those who greet him at the close of the service murmur words like *beautiful* and *inspirational,* and the coffee hour is all sweetness and light. But when he finally puts on his coat and makes his way out of the church he spots a furtive character lurking in the doorway, the sight of whom immediately extinguishes the inward glow. For he knows almost exactly what this stranger is going to tell him. The stranger is stranded in New York, with a sick wife waiting for him in Albany, Chicago, or San Francisco (according to his estimate of the pastor's resources). And, of course, on a Sunday all the agencies of relief are closed.

What does the preacher do? The tempting response is to do a quick reverse and exit by another door. Then, unless his skin is especially thick, his conscience will prick him all the way home as phrases from his sermon rise up to torment him and charge him with hypocrisy. The same thing may happen if he stops and listens to the story, then coldly informs the supplicant that there is nothing he can do. But if, on the other hand, he listens sympathetically and then hands over money with a smile and a blessing, can he then be sure that he has done the right thing and put his sermon into practice? Conscience again says: "Ah! Easy way out; and you have just contributed to the downfall of a panhandler who will proceed to milk another pastor even less able to afford it. Is that Christian love?"

Well, what's the answer? I simply raise the question to illustrate the fact that it is not only the man in the pew who finds difficulty in translating the fine words into appropriate action. Every one of us knows of the tension that exists between the rhetoric and the reality of Christian love. There is no problem more agonizing for the Church today than the widespread notion that what we hear and pray and sing in church has little to do with the decisions we have to make in business, in politics, in chance encounters, or even in the home. The rhetoric of the pulpit seems to belong to a happy land, far, far away, where all agree that love is wonderful and where it sounds as if we are called to make a simple choice between what is clearly right and what is certainly wrong. But the reality is that the way of love is often much more worrisome than wonderful, and the choice seldom seems as black and white as it sounds in church.

This contrast hit me forcibly when as a young preacher I was a chaplain in a prisoner of war camp. In circumstances of close confinement and enforced proximity there is little chance that mere rhetoric will be greeted with pious enthusiasm. Every statement was under scrutiny by men who shared the same privations and were exposed to the same temptations as the preacher. There's nothing like intimate contact day by day and night by night for throttling down the oratory! I'm not saying that we found the Christian Gospel unworkable and ineffective. On the contrary the New Testament came to life on occasion much as Ernest Gordon has described in his moving book *Through the Valley of the Kwai*, where a prison church was born through a reading of the Gospels. But we learned something of the tough decisions love requires.

Suppose you are in a little cell with three others and normally eat at a little table opposite one of them. The authorities decide not to issue daily bread, but to give each prisoner a loaf to last the week. You measure off a seventh and put the remainder carefully away each day. The man opposite you does what we'd all long to do—bolts the entire loaf on the first day. After two or three days, as he watches you consume your allotted portion, do you give him some, thus ensuring he'll do the same thing next time around? Or, let's say, you are fortunate enough one day to receive a private parcel from Switzerland containing a slab of chocolate. Divided among two hundred it would mean nothing, but divided among four it would be a treat for all. Or do you go into a quiet corner and consume the lot? Perhaps this case is easier—but you can see how on occasion a sermon would come home to roost.

The first thing I have to say about this tension between our Christian ideals and practice is this: If you are troubled by the contrast between the rhetoric and the reality, if you are often puzzled about the really loving course of action, then thank God! The most devastating disease that can infect a church or a Christian soul is a paralysis of conscience, an inability to see where we fall short or the comfortable conviction that there is no real agony of decision. The real Christian is not the one who is satisfied with his level of performance and tells you glibly that he lives by the Sermon on the Mount. (It is usually the non-churchgoer who makes that remark!) The real Christian knows what it means to confess failures in love and to pray to God in his mercy to "forgive what we have been, amend what we are, and direct what we shall be."

This means that we realize the way of love is no soft and sentimental road, and that it offers no easy answers. But it also means that we believe in an inexhaustible grace that forgives our failures and constantly empowers us to do better. That is the liberating hope of the Gospel that reaches us when we need it. For our love, we know, is exhaustible. That is why I am concentrating now on just one aspect of love—our tendency to get tired, to compromise, and to settle for something less than the demands of Jesus.

Jesus' commandment of love is not a kind of blind benevolence that sees no evil and tries to smother everyone in a genial embrace. It is a commandment precisely because it can be obeyed by an act of will, but no act of will can enable me to like everybody that crosses my path, or to feel emotionally drawn to them. The love Jesus teaches and exemplifies is a strong and resolute desire for the welfare of others, a refusal to indulge in hatred or revenge, a willingness to forgive again and again, and concern—even for our opponents—meaning we desire nothing but good for them. Dr. William Barclay has summed up Jesus' message like this: "It would be impossible to demand that we love our enemies as we love those who are dearer to us than love itself. But it is possible to say to us: 'You must try to be like God. You must try never to wish anything but good for others. You must try to look at every man with the eyes of God, with the eyes of goodwill.' "

This is how Jesus' life dazzled and astonished the world. The Gospels don't show us a mild and mushy idealist, who speaks of a fantasy world in which everyone is lovable. He was a strong character who "knew what was in man" (John 2:25) and was not afraid to call a spade a spade—as when he referred to Herod Antipas as "that fox" (Luke 13:32). But with all his insight into the evil around him and what it might eventually do to him, he unswervingly sought the best for every man, woman, and child who crossed his path, without regard for their worthiness in the eyes of men. His love never tired, even when the establishment unleashed its fury against him, or when his friends disappointed him by their frailty and folly and deserted him in his hour of need. From the agony of the cross he looked down at the taunting priests, the callous soldiers, and the bloodthirsty crowd and cried: "Father, forgive them; for

they know not what they do" (Luke 23:34). And, as for the
disciples who were cowering in their hiding places, we
learn that "having loved his own which were in the world,
he loved them unto the end."

Jesus never ceased to commend this kind of love to his
disciples with a wealth of startling illustrations and epi-
grams. Since he knew well how easily we lose heart when
we try to practice care and concern, he shocked his disciples with the remark: "If your brother wrongs you, rebuke
him; and, if he repents, forgive him. Even if he wrongs you
seven times in a day and comes back to you seven times,
saying, 'I am sorry,' you are to forgive him" (Luke 17:4).
Here he's obviously not talking about someone whom it is
easy to love and to forgive. Recently I received a letter in
which a social worker friend wrote of the difference between the "attractive" sinner, or person with a problem,
and the "chronic" who tries your patience. "How your heart
sinks," she wrote, "when a certain person asks for an ap-
pointment or phones." Here Jesus is surely talking about the
chronic. How long are we supposed to go on accepting,
forgiving, trying to help? The answer, in the form of the
mystic number seven, is "forever."

Notice that in the case where real wrong has been
done to you Jesus doesn't gloss over the fault. He uses the
words rebuke and repent. Love involves an element of
toughness in dealing with the chronic. How else would love
seek the best for him? We must avoid not only anger and
rejection, but simply giving up. Like Jesus, we are to love
unto the end. This applies, not just to people whom we call
"problem cases," but to the most intimate relationships in
the home or at work. We must go on loving even the
difficult person in this way. Paul tells us in his exquisite
interpretation of the love of Christ: "Love is patient; love is
kind and envies no one. Love is never boastful nor conceit-
ed, nor rude; never selfish, not quick to take offense. Love
keeps no score of wrongs; does not gloat over other men's
sins . . ." (1 Cor. 13:4, 5).

If we really hear that, we can understand Jesus' words

about continuing to forgive. But it is possible to accept this commandment in a smug and self-satisfied way, assuming that all wrong is on the other side. I sometimes get letters in which people write about their constant forbearance and forgiveness of an erring spouse or child, while assuming that their own behavior is immaculate. As in such counseling problems I want equal time for the other party. "Love keeps no score of wrongs."

This is a tough assignment. The disciples were overwhelmed. And their response is striking. "Lord," they said, "increase our faith." That's a little odd at first sight; you would expect them to say "increase our love." But there it is: "Increase our faith." It's worth pondering that this expression doesn't come after Jesus has been speaking about matters of doctrine and belief. If he had, for example, been expounding the dogma of the Trinity or the mystery of his person, it would have been natural for them to ask for an increase of faith. But it was when they were faced with the demands of an absolute and untiring love that they made this request.

At least they had begun to see what Jesus meant by faith, a discovery that many still have to make. For he had made it clear that faith is trust in a God of total and untiring love. The more we know and rely on God—who is willing to accept us as we are, who doesn't demand that we reach a certain level of goodness in order to be forgiven, who loves as indiscriminately as the rain that falls on the just and the unjust, and who works in everything for good with them that love him—the more we shall be empowered to love and keep on loving.

This is why we can never separate, as some try to do, the ethics and the devotion of the Christian way. The demands of this untiring love are impossible without the sustaining grace of God, from whom it flows. From the beginning, Christians were able to demonstrate this love to an astonished world because they were in constant touch with the loving God, looking to his Son for inspiration, and knowing the indwelling power of his Spirit. That is what we must do as we return to the hard task of loving the unlovable, caring for the unattractive, and refusing to give up on the difficult and demanding. Most of all we need an increase in our faith in the God who treats you and me just like that. There is no better way to increase that faith than to center our lives in prayer, worship, and devotion to Jesus Christ. "Think of him," said the apostle, "who submitted to such opposition from sinners: that will help you not to lose heart and grow faint" (Hab. 12:3).

We confess, O Lord, that we do not find it easy to love like Jesus, that too often our love gets tired. Draw us closer to him that we may catch the infection of his immense caring for all kinds of people. Let his spirit more and more rule within us so that we may practice the forgiveness of those who have been forgiven, and have the patience and realism that faith in him inspires. Amen.

10

Do We Have to Be Zealous?

From occasional remarks that people make to me I get the impression that what troubles them about many religious movements and church activities is the constant demand for zeal and enthusiasm. They seem to be saying: "Why can't I just be a simple believer, saying my prayers, supporting good causes, and attending church when I want to without being badgered to join crusades, demonstrate my convictions, and evangelize all over the place? That's not my style. I've got my own kind of faith, so leave me alone!"

There was a time when I would have dismissed such remarks as evidence of a lukewarm faith and a lack of real commitment to the Christian cause, but I now have more sympathy for this point of view. It's not that I want to settle for a half-hearted discipleship or to plead for a tepid, compromising kind of religion, but that I've had second thoughts about zeal. From the Bible and from experience I have learned that religious zeal is not always a good thing. Many sincere believers are bewildered by the constant demand to be more zealous, and many thoughtful inquirers are held back from Christian commitment by the thought that they will be expected to be fanatically devoted to the cause.

Today, the message resounds from a thousand pulpits:

Wake up! Get moving! Be involved! Pray more! Love more! Give more! We live under the sign of the exclamation mark. Preachers have become barkers, urging people to participate, to worship, and to become totally committed. Those who have been at least zealous enough to come to worship often find themselves under the lash, and when the benediction comes they take with them a guilty conscience rather than the peace of God that passes all understanding. Then there are those millions who are not at all sure of their faith, are perhaps in quest of a faith that has somehow eluded them, and are somewhat scared of the image of the fervent disciple. They would like to know God and be inspired by the Spirit of Christ, but have an aversion to anything that smells of religious fanaticism. It is these people I have in mind when I ask, "Do we have to be zealous?"

My own faith needs to hear the call to be zealous in order to challenge my spiritual indolence and the desire to avoid the real cost of discipleship. I believe, too, that in many of our so-called main-line churches there is a lack of zeal, a consequence of settling for a religion that makes no demands. The season of Lent is designed to make us reckon with our indulgence in a soft Christianity and should arouse us to a reckoning with the Lord we profess to follow. Are we not often shamed by those who are intensely active propagating religions in which we do not believe? Why are we so reticent about sharing the good news that our Lord has committed to us? We say we don't want to become fanatical, but is there no line to be drawn between the genuine enthusiast and the fanatic? Were the apostles fanatical? Was Jesus?

Questions like these drove me to the Bible, where I found some fascinating insights that I want to try to pass on. I discovered that zeal in itself is by no means universally commended in the Bible. "The zeal of thy house hath eaten me up" (Ps. 69:9), said the psalmist, referring to his enthusiasm for the worship of God. This phrase was echoed by the disciples when they watched Jesus cleansing the temple, and refers to the inspired zeal for purity and sincerity in adoration of God and response to his word. But not all zeal for the Lord is viewed positively in the Bible. Paul remarks about some of his former associates: "To their zeal for God I can testify; but it is an ill-informed zeal" (Rom. 10:2). And surely "ill-informed zeal" is the least that can be said about the activities of Jehu in the Old Testament. "Come with me," he said, "and see my zeal for the Lord"—and then proceeded to one bloody massacre after another. Wasn't it the zeal of the disciples that led them to say: "Master, we saw a man driving out devils in your name, and as he was not one of us, we tried to stop him"? And Jesus blasted this intolerant zeal with the restraining words: "He who is not against us is on our side" (Luke 9:49,50).

The question arises: Was Jesus zealous? If by zeal we mean a total devotion to the will of God, a giving on behalf of others, and a passionate desire for the liberation of human beings from all that enslaves and degrades, then no greater zeal has ever been seen on earth. But if by zeal we mean a ferocious appetite for converts, thrusting of one's beliefs on others, and tactless and insensitive intrusion into their private lives, then there was no such zeal in him. He was not a crusading knight in shining armor trampling down the opposition, but came among us as a servant, and the symbol of his presence was not a tyrant but a child. His burning message and his healing powers are not described in the Gospels as deployed in a mighty mass movement to corral men and women like cattle into the kingdom. Rather we read of individuals, each one different, and each one respected as a person, who came in touch with him, usually at their own request. There is no doubt about his summons to his disciples for a total commitment of body, mind, and spirit to his cause. Yet there are also times when he seems to be giving them the advice that the French statesman Talleyrand gave an aspiring diplomat: "Surtout, pas trop de zele." ("Above all, not too much zeal.") There is a zeal that loses sight of Christ in a self-centered effort to advocate his cause. That's what happened to the disciples once when they suggested that the best way to treat a village that had rejected him was to call down fire from heaven. George Santayana defined zealotry as: "When a man loses his aim and redoubles his effort."

There is a striking quote about zeal in the Book of Revelation: "Be zealous and repent." "Be zealous," we read. Yes, be zealous, you Church of Laodicea. (Have you ever been a member of it?) "I know thy words, that thou are neither cold nor hot: I would that thou wert cold or hot. So then because thou art lukewarm, and neither cold nor hot, I will spue thee out of my mouth" (Rev. 3:16). It takes language like that to rouse us from the half-hearted discipleship into which we so easily slip—lukewarm worship, flimsy prayers, feeble service, and token pledges. It shocks us into realizing that we cannot announce that "Jesus Christ is my Lord and Savior" and then treat him and his Church as of minor importance in the rhythm of our busy lives. There may come a time, as our powers wane, and we near the end of our mortal days, when we might have to say, with Shakespeare's Thomas Cromwell:

> Had I but served my God with half the zeal
> I served my king, he would not in mine age
> Have left me naked to mine enemies.
>
> (Henry VIII:III. 2, 456)

Have we a king we serve—success, comfort, money, self-indulgence—with greater zeal than Christ?

"Be zealous and repent." Here is the secret of Christian zeal. At first, this may conjure up a picture of zealous repenting, an orgy of breast-beating, a spectacular scene of sack-cloth and ashes. But these words mean something quite different and offer a clue to this question of being zealous.

Repentance, in the Bible, does not mean a sporadic outpouring of sorrow for our sins. It is the condition of being turned away from self and toward God. It is not a once-and-for-all event in which we confess our need for a Savior, but an attitude of mind and spirit. The New Testament defines a Christian as one who repents, believes, and lives constantly in the atmosphere of the publican at prayer: "God be merciful to me a sinner." To live with repentance and to rely on God's grace, therefore, defines and qualifies the way in which we express our zeal.

To repent is to be humble inside. Such humility is a protection against the zeal of the fanatic or the arrogant. There was no such humility in the religious people Jesus denounced when he said: "Woe unto you . . . for ye compass sea and land to make one proselyte, and when he is made, ye make him twofold more the child of hell than yourselves" (Matt. 23:15). The zeal of the Christian evangelist, for instance, is not that of one who claims to be superior and demands that others become like him. It is the enthusiasm of one who says: "I want to share with you the news of a Savior whom I really need."

When we repent and become aware that it's not our brand of religion but Christ alone who saves us, we will be delivered from obsessive preoccupation with ourselves. It is this that gives the true saints their extraordinary freedom and joy. Repentance, believe it or not, breeds a sense of humor. The zealot, the grim-faced, wild-eyed proselytizer, has none. Nor, on the other hand, does the person who reacts angrily to the zealot, and hates any kind of religious commitment. Both take themselves too seriously. To repent is really a way of learning to laugh at oneself.

Fundamentally, we are talking about living by grace. When Paul talked about those who had a zeal for God, "but not an informed zeal," he was speaking of those who believed they could work their way into the Kingdom of God. Their zeal was to save themselves. And there are many, even within the churches, who are driven by the thought that they must work their passage, that they must prove and justify themselves by their energy in good causes. As Paul would say, "They have fallen from grace." That is the original meaning of that phrase. When we fall from grace we may well begin trying to prove ourselves by our zeal. And that is the recipe for a zeal that goes sour.

The following passage from the Book of Revelation brings us the one and only secret of true Christian zeal. It is the unforgettable image of Jesus himself knocking at the door of our hearts—the Lord, the Master, the Son of God, waiting like a suppliant to be admitted. Here is Jesus, in whose body are the marks of the only zeal he demands from his followers—the zeal of love. "Behold, I stand at the door and knock" (Rev. 3:20).

Don't you sometimes feel that you want to say with John Donne: "Batter my heart, three-personed God!" so that your will is broken and your life remade? But no. Grace comes as the latch is lifted. "If any man hear my voice and open the door, I will come in."

Do we have to be zealous? Yes, zealous with a zeal of love, which cannot be induced by threat or exhortation but is the spontaneous response of those who open up their lives to the company of Christ. To meet with him, to sup with him, to share his love—this is the source and center of the joyful and spontaneous zeal that should mark our lives as Christians.

When we are tired and half-hearted, Lord, refresh us with the zeal of thy burning love; when we are over-confident and opinionated guard us from the zeal of fanaticism and make us humble. At all times keep us within the circle of thy care and mold us in the image of Jesus Christ our Lord. Amen.

11

Who Could Be Against Jesus?

At this time of the year I often find myself wondering about the grim part of the Christian story, the way in which Jesus was treated during the final weeks of his mortal life. What bothers me is the conflict between the clear record that almost everyone turned against him, and the modern assumption that nearly everyone admires Jesus and has nothing but good to say about him. Are we so much better, more sensitive, more humane, and more appreciative of sheer goodness than the people of Palestine two thousand years ago? In some ways, perhaps, but in general there is as much hatred, fear, corruption, and brutality now as then. If we say that no one is against Jesus now, may it not be that we haven't really understood what it was that brought him to his cross?

Suppose for a moment that you are reading one of the Gospels for the first time and have never before heard anything about Jesus. Let's imagine that you've read about halfway through. You have heard about a Jesus who spent himself on behalf of others, bringing hope to the despondent, courage to the weak, health to the sick, peace to the possessed, and a sense of forgiveness to the guilt-ridden. He seems to have been totally free from inhibition about the rank, race, or social reputation of the people he met. He accepted everyone, from the rich and the learned to the poor and the outcast, simply on the basis of human need. He didn't attach himself to any of the subversive movements of the day and thus alarm the Roman authorities. Nor did he attempt to form any break-away religious group, and thus alarm the ecclesiastical authorities. He stayed within the law and observed the religious duties of Judaism as laid down in the Scriptures. His sermons and stories about the kingdom of God puzzled many people, but, on the whole, he seems to have been immensely popular with the common people.

Suppose now that, having read halfway through the Gospel, and being one of those people who can't resist peaking into the last chapter of a detective story, you slip over the pages and suddenly find yourself reading the story of the crucifixion. Wouldn't you be surprised and horrified? How could this be the fate of a man whose life was devoted to preaching good news, to healing the sick, and to releasing men, women, and children from demonic forces? Or— more puzzling still—how could this be the destiny of the Son of God, who claims to have come to bring people into the family of the Father in heaven? Wouldn't you want to look for some clues in the story that might help answer these questions? I suggest that a careful reading of the story, of the words and actions of Jesus, and of the response of different sections of the population, might reveal to us the answer to the haunting question, "Who could be against Jesus?"

First, I am struck by the fact that in the early chapters of the Gospels Jesus is shown to be avoiding as much as possible the adulation of the crowds and the leadership role they seem to be thrusting upon him. We keep reading about his going away. An alarming story about the execution of John the Baptist is followed by Jesus' words to his disciples who had just returned from an exciting missionary tour: "Let us go off by ourselves to some place where we will be alone" (Mark 6:31). But he has trouble shaking off the

crowds, and you sense in these passages the tension between his desire to avoid the pressure of the crowd and his
tremendous compassion. When he tried to escape by boat,
the crowd swarmed around the lake on foot and waited for
him on the other side. Instead of being furious, like a
modern celebrity dodging the microphones and cameras,
"His heart," we read "was filled with pity for them, because they were like sheep without a shepherd" (Mark
6:34). So he fed them. Then he managed to get the crowds
away and "went to a hill to pray."

Then we find him moving about the country a great
deal, never staying long enough anywhere for a mass movement to form behind him. He discourages any talk about
his being Messiah. Why?

One reason relates to the Roman authorities, who could
easily become his dangerous enemy. Already there was
enough being said out loud, and whispered in the back-
streets, about the successor to John the Baptist to make the
Romans jumpy. And it was a Roman procurator, in the end,
who was to sign Jesus' death warrant. But there is a more
important reason for the reluctance of Jesus to rouse the
crowds. You can be against Jesus, or his church, because
you see him as a menace to the established order. You can
also be against him when you misinterpret his message and
the meaning of his kingdom. He seems to have sensed in
the attitude of the crowds what you might call religion for
the wrong reasons. The Fourth Gospel tells us that after the
miracle of the loaves and fishes Jesus said to the crowd:
"You are looking for me now not because you saw my signs
but because you ate the food and had all you wanted" (John
6:26). We are all subject to the temptation to use religion for
our own satisfaction. Popular religion from that day to the
present has tended to sell faith to the crowds as the answer
to immediate needs. I keep getting mailings from evangelists
who offer me not only health and peace of mind, but
prosperity, good luck, and increased income, in return for a
request for prayer and a suitable contribution. It is hard for
us to understand that we are against Jesus if we seek from

him what we most desire rather than what he has to give us. He wants to give us God's presence, the knowledge of his will, and the grace to live with it. When he saw that the crowds want something else, he realized how quickly that could turn them from being adoring listeners to howling for his blood.

It is during this period that Jesus revealed himself more and more to those who were closest to him. Time and again he took the disciples apart, and at least three times he tells them of his coming trial and death. At the same time as he speaks of his rejection, there are increasing revelations of the mystery of his being Son of God. With the disciples alone in a storm-tossed boat he speaks a majestic word of calm. To the disciples, afloat in the middle of the night, he comes, walking on the water. And only Peter, James and John had that momentary vision of his divinity, that foretaste of his Resurrection we call the Transfiguration. It is as though Jesus was telling those who had eyes to see and ears to hear: "Look! Listen! This is the kind of Christ I am—not the political leader that some want, not the miracle-worker who satisfied the crowd, not the avenging Messiah who burns up the wicked and sets up his kingdom with invincible force, but the Son of God who is willing to suffer in order to liberate the world." And when Peter would have none of it Jesus did not hesitate to call him an enemy: "Get away from me, Satan. Your thoughts are men's thoughts, not God's!" (Matt. 16:23).

I spoke once in a sermon about the "dumb disciples of Jesus." Mark's Gospel tells us again and again how slow the disciples were to see what he meant, and how obtuse they were in understanding his spirit. Are we too not capable of being against Jesus—even when we think we are being his disciples? These men got into a boat with Jesus and immediately started worrying about the lack of provisions. And Jesus said: "Why are you discussing not having any bread? Don't you know or understand yet? Are your minds so dull? You have eyes—can't you see? You have ears—can't you hear?" (Mark 8:17). Then he reminded them of the miracle of abundance, the multiplication of the loaves. Do you and I never find ourselves worrying about the future and the provision for ourselves and those whom we love? And have we not also fed at the Lord's table and heard the words: "He who comes to me shall not hunger"? Haven't we also at times sought from Jesus the things he has not come to give, and rejected the very things he offers? Aren't we working against Jesus when we want him to work our kind of miracle, not his?

Now I want to turn to a remark of Jesus which comes almost as a parenthesis in the story of the boat and the bread. Under his breath we hear Jesus saying: "Look out, and be on your guard against the yeast of the Pharisees and the yeast of Herod." He has already identified two parties in the land who are definitely against him—the Pharisees and the Herodians. He sees their influence spreading across the land like yeast, or leaven (the familiar word in this context). It is surprising that Jesus should mention the two in one breath, for they loathed and distrusted one another. It is as if he had a premonition that, in the end, it would be a sudden and unnatural alliance between these groups that would bring him to the place where the ultimate civil authority, wielded by the Romans, would slay him.

Who were these Pharisees, and why were they against him? Mark's use of the word to denote people who were fanatical defenders of the external rites of religion but inwardly corrupt, hard-hearted, and proud led to the word *Pharisee* being used in common speech as the equivalent of *hypocrite*. This is unfair to a sect of Judaism that did much to preserve its great traditions during a period of laxity and demoralization. Many of the Pharisees of Jesus' day were among the most devout and courageous, and the Gospels tell of men like Nicodemus who were most responsive to the message of Jesus. When Jesus warned of "the yeast of the Pharisees" he was talking of one particular group that had resisted him from the beginning, that had attacked him for his compassionate disregard for the Sabbath laws, that had objected to the low company he kept, and finally saw him as a deceiver of the common people whom they were trying to keep in line.

No one can be more vicious than a man or woman fanatically devoted to a body of religious beliefs and rules, and lacking the grace of compassion, or that aid to humility we call a sense of humor. The record of cruelty perpetrated by this kind of pharisaism, particularly within the Christian Church, is atrocious. In the name of Jesus, things have been said and done in flagrant denial of his spirit. No matter how loudly a person may speak the name of Jesus, if he acts without humility, grace, and compassion, he is Jesus' enemy.

In attacking this perverted religion of outward forms and rigid rules, Jesus stood in the line of the great Hebrew prophets. He quotes from Isaiah the burning words: "These people, says God, honor me with their words, but their heart is really far away from me" (Mark 7:6). Who could be against Jesus? Who could actually hate this man who spoke of God's kingdom, who healed, and who banished the demons? Only, apparently, those whose brand of religion was offended by his offer of salvation to all and sundry, by his healing done on the Sabbath day, and by one who was thought by some to be an exorcist in league with the devil to do such things. That is the record. It was the hyperreligious—not the scallywags, the harlots, or the rough Roman soldiers—who were furiously against Jesus.

Is there nothing in us today that, perhaps secretly, corresponds to this hostility to Jesus? Do we never find ourselves longing for a quiet and orderly religion that will not be disturbed by the flaming demands of Christ's love? Are we easily outraged by persons or movements that seem to threaten the religious structure in which we feel secure? Is it possible that we too may let the religious institution or our code of moral behavior at times smother the spirit of Jesus? You and I know the answer to these questions, so once again we must look within. We are not here to judge the Pharisees, who worked like yeast to permeate the people with their antagonism to Jesus, but to unveil and expel the Pharisaism in our own heart.

What was that other yeast working against Jesus, the Herodians? The Herod who had John the Baptist's head cut off was not the Herod who ordered the massacre of the innocents; nor was he the Herod whose spectacular death is described in the Book of the Acts; nor was he the Herod before whom the Apostle Paul appeared. If this confuses you it doesn't matter, for all the Herods were equally obnoxious and corrupt. The one who had John the Baptist's head cut off was Herod Antipas, the tetrarch of Galilee. He was half-Jewish and ruled by favor of the Roman emperor with whom he was careful to keep on good terms. The political party that supported him in his policy of détente with the Romans had the name "Herodians," and from the Gospels we can derive a rough picture of the kind of people they were. Herod himself stood for a life of personal amorality and public pragmatism and cynicism. In other words, he was privately a rogue and politically a twister. Jesus, according to Luke, once referred to him in passing as "that fox." This puppet-king represented a way of life that was totally opposed to that of the Pharisees, and also totally opposed to the mission of Jesus.

Those who were against Jesus included not only the fanatically and rigidly religious but also those who didn't give a damn about the kingdom of God, laughed at the moral demands of the Sermon on the Mount, and carved out for themselves a kingdom of sensuality, profligacy, extravagance, and vice.

The Herodians were not all as vicious or as successful as Herod Antipas, the spirit of amorality, corruption, cynicism, and irreligion worked like yeast throughout the realm. And such yeast, then as now, is the enemy of Jesus. It is time we noticed how this yeast is operating in our own society. We are aware of crime, corruption, and the slipping moral standards, but do we see how subtly cynicism, materialism, and ethical compromises can infect us all? Do we plainly see the spirit of the Herodians as the enemy of Jesus? We have been accustomed to the thought of a Christian society where God is acknowledged, the ideals of Jesus reverenced, and certain standards universally accepted, if not always kept. So it is not easy for us to think of this trend as plainly anti-Christian. But the Herodians are here, and their yeast is working. That is why we have such a need for the tremendous yeast of the kingdom of God and the Church as a catalyst in society working for the way of Christ.

These, then, are some of the answers to the question: who can be against Jesus? We can follow him on that last journey to Jerusalem and see him on his cross only if we realize the subtle forces around us, and in us, that really oppose him. May we experience this Lent the expulsive power of his sacrificial love in our own hearts, and accept the challenge to be always on his side.

Make us aware, O God, of the ways in which we oppose the will of Jesus and deny him by our words and deeds. Give us a spirit of repentance and readiness to hear again his challenge to take up our cross and follow him who is our way, our truth, and our life. Amen.

12

On the Road with Jesus

I wonder if you do most of your thinking with words or with pictures? We all use both but some are more inclined to one rather than the other. If I leave my study to go and look up a telephone number in the outer office of my church, I come back muttering 289-4403 (or whatever it is), and unless I remember these words I'm sunk. My wife, on the other hand, sees the number in a picture and has no trouble in reproducing it. I suppose that since a preacher deals constantly with words—other people's words in books and articles and his own words as he writes and speaks—he tends to do most of his thinking with words. So we run the risk of overestimating the place of words, ideas, arguments, and proofs in the field of religion.

But this division is not absolute. Words themselves can form pictures, and I find that some of the most powerful influences in my own life as a believer come from various such word-pictures. I can't help noticing, too, that the Bible is very much more like an art gallery than a philosophical library. It's full of word-pictures, and nowhere more than in the Gospels. Most Christians have in their heads a number of the sayings of Jesus, but my guess is that they are more influenced by various pictures that come to mind from the Gospel stories.

One such picture has etched itself into my mind, and I want to show it to you today. It has to do with the Lenten story of Jesus' journey to Jerusalem to face his enemies and risk the cross. In Mark's Gospel the picture is, for me, unforgettable. This is what Mark says about the beginning of the journey: "They were on the road, going up to Jerusalem, Jesus leading the way; and the disciples were filled with awe; while those who followed behind were afraid" (Mark 10:32). It's not a very glorious picture, is it? We don't see a triumphant band of disciples marching on Jerusalem with drums beating and flags flying. But it's a very vivid picture, and perhaps we can find ourselves in it more easily than in something grandiose.

In the earlier chapters we see Jesus moving erratically about the countryside, avoiding the crowds in Galilee, trying to be alone with his disciples, evidently aware of the growing power of his enemies. His disciples, like passengers in a plane on a foggy day circling above the airport, were anxious and confused; and like such passengers when the plane finally descends and zeroes in on the runway, they were both relieved and alarmed. Their pilot had made up his mind. Jesus was striding ahead like one who knew exactly where he was going. His mind was made up. Luke, always the more elegant writer, puts it like this: "As the time approached when he was to be taken up to heaven, he set his face resolutely towards Jerusalem, and sent messengers ahead" (Luke 9:51). Whoever told Luke about this decisive moment in the story must have caught that look in Jesus' face. "He set his face" is a Semitic expression implying utter determination.

This Jesus who outpaces his laggard disciples on the Jerusalem road is not the soft and tender character about whom we sing so often in our hymns. (I sometimes wonder why hymn-writers are obsessed with the word *sweet* when referring to Jesus when *tough* would often be more appropriate—perhaps it's easier to find a rhyme.) He has come from God to lead us to God. He has immense compassion and understanding for our human frailties. But he goes head-on toward the enemy, knowing well the malignity of the powers of evil that surround us all, and demonstrating that the path to victory goes rough and through the thorns of suffering. It is this real Jesus, who deliberately took the rough road to Jerusalem, who can brace us for our own encounter with our enemies and keep our eyes on the city of God. Toward the end of World War II, I preached on Palm Sunday, 1945, in a stalag in Germany to men who knew, as I did, that within a few days we should be either dead or liberated. And the text that came to my mind, the text I gave them, was just this, that "Jesus set his face to go to Jerusalem." That's the kind of Savior he is—the Son of God who has been there, who knows, and who can bring us through, whatever.

The disciples, at this time, were a few steps behind. They were in no hurry to reach Jerusalem. The King James Version says, "they were amazed"; the New English Bible, "they were filled with awe." If there is one thing missing in most of our contemporary pictures of Jesus—the popular paintings, the folksongs, the movies, and the books—it is this note of awe. We seem to want a Jesus we can fully understand, one about whom there is no ultimate mystery, a "regular guy." But he was an "irregular guy"; totally one of us, yet uniquely one with the "immortal, invisible God only wise." That is why I turn from the shimmering pictures of modern Church publications, not to the theatricality of Dali, but to the dark splendor of a Rouault or an icon. The Jesus we find in Mark's Gospel is intensely human, but there is something about him that evokes our wonder, our awe, and even at times our fear.

I think it is his goodness that evokes these feelings in us. The question he fired at the rich young man, "Why do you call me good?" was surely meant to raise the word *good* from a conventional compliment to an overpowering challenge. Why do we call him good? Isn't it because we are aware of him as one who lived completely within the will of God and who never for a moment lets us forget the supreme demands of God's kingdom? There is, for us, something awe-inspiring about his refusal to let anything come between us and the perfect will of God. Two incidents in this same chapter of the Bible illustrate his almost terrifying emphasis on the perfect standards of the kingdom. They have to do with the two areas where we feel the tensions between our normal practice and the precepts of God—sex and money. His words about divorce and about the danger of riches are not some new law binding on his followers. He is not legislating that there shall be no more divorce and that every Christian must divest himself of all his property and income. He is simply saying, as he did throughout the Sermon on the Mount, that it is the will of God that marriage is the union of two people for life, and that money must never usurp God's place in our love and worship.

It is this kind of goodness that is awe-inspiring. No wonder the disciples responded with: "Who, then, can be saved?" No wonder they lagged behind when this Lord strode forward on the Jerusalem road. And no wonder "the people who followed behind," the fringe who like many today were attracted but not yet ready to be his disciples, "were afraid." Sex and money, more than ever, are the rival gods for our worship today. And the challenge of one who accepted both as powerful and natural expressions of our humanity, subordinated to the claims of God's kingdom, was awe-inspiring.

But if this had been all that they found in Jesus would they have kept on following after him on the Jerusalem road? Would they not have straggled off, one by one, to pick up the threads of their humdrum, not-so-good lives, and let him forge ahead by himself, this man who was too good to live? Something held them as it holds us whenever we are tempted to throw aside the demands of Jesus and settle for a less strenuous ethic and a more comfortable religion. What holds us is the overwhelming impression that this man knows us through and through, yet never gives up on the belief that, with all our fears and hesitations, we can still enter his kingdom and know what it is to be sons and daughters of God. He brushes aside the feeling of helplessness and hopelessness that sweeps over anyone who is dismayed by his ideal of goodness. "Who, then, can be saved?" "Jesus looked straight at them [as he is looking straight at you and me] and answered, 'This is impossible for men, but not for God; everything is possible for God.'" He believed it was possible for God to take our stumbling feet and set them on the right path; to take our mixed-up lives and straighten them out by his grace; to take our fears and wash them out by his love. "Everything is possible for God" (Matt. 19:25,26).

So they followed him, not because they felt equal to the task of being his disciples, but because they found in him the divine possibility of new life and hope. They followed him because his ultimate word to them was not: "Do this; do that; or you can't be my disciples"; but "come to me and I will refresh you; come as you are and I will forgive you; come like a child and I will instruct you." They had seen the children swarming around Jesus; and just when they were trying to drive them away, he had opened his arms wide in welcome, put his hands on each one of them, and blessed them. "This is how you will have to come," he had said. "Whoever does not receive the Kingdom of God like a child will never enter it." There's no word about innocence here. You and I can't become innocent, and I'm sure Jesus had no illusions about the angelic goodness of little children. It's dependence he is talking about, helplessness, and trust. Even the most sophisticated enter the kingdom on a level with the dumbest, and the rich enter the kingdom on a level with the poor. Years ago, Dr. Barnardo's Home opened in England as an orphanage with the motto, "No destitute child ever refused admission," and that is still the motto of the kingdom of God. The disciples were drawn after Jesus on the Jerusalem road because they sensed in him the welcome of God once they abandoned their pretensions and admitted that they were destitute. Like Peter on another occasion, they saw no other hope: "Lord, to whom shall we go: you have the words of eternal life" (John 6:68).

So they followed. And Jesus told them what was going to happen to him, and warned that they too would know something of the suffering involved in following his way. You might think that after all this they would have learned what it means to take the road with Jesus—that it is a road of humility, dependence, and service to others. Yet what happened? Immediately after his solemn words about the cross, they began maneuvering for positions of eminence in the coming glory. James and John came up with a request. "What do you want me to do for you?" asks Jesus. "When you sit on your throne in the glorious kingdom, we want you to let us sit with you, one at your right hand and one at your left" (Mark 10:36,37). The other disciples got wind of this request and were furious. Soon the surrounding rocks echoed with a terrible argument about status and prestige, while Jesus moved firmly on to his humiliation and his cross.

We don't learn the lesson of humility once for all, and it's not for us to scoff at the dumb disciples. Again and again, Lent after Lent, Good Friday after Good Friday, day after day, we have to meet Jesus on his way to Jerusalem, and hear the amazing words: "Even the Son of Man did not come to be served; he came to serve and to give his life to redeem many people" (Mark 10:45). He is inviting us to take this road again with him. He does so very personally. What I find so moving in the Jesus we meet in the Gospels is the way he brings both his demands and his amazing grace to each individual. "He took the children in his arms, placed his hands on each of them, and blessed them." Of the rich young ruler Mark says that "Jesus looked straight at him with love." He spoke bluntly to Peter, James, and John, who were all obsessed with their absurd ambition, and said: "What do you want me to do for you?" In a strange way every single one found his reflection in the heart of Jesus, and he responded to each individual's need. He was not the spiritual autocrat drumming up disciples to march like robots into his kingdom: "What do you want me to do for you?" Their answer to his question tells him who they are, and his response reveals their greater need.

So Jesus marches on, with his disciples straggling a little behind, all filled with awe and wonder at this extraordinary leader who is taking them they know not where. And further behind is a crowd of people, still attracted by the young preacher and healer, but increasingly afraid of what he is getting them into. When a country is prosperous and churches are flourishing no one is afraid to sign up as a disciple. In the 1950s church membership in this country rose to an all-time high. But when the going gets rough those who stay with the Christian community are more likely to be the ones who have glimpsed what it really means to be a disciple. Then is the time for this picture of Jesus striding on ahead, of the awe in the eyes of his disciples, and fear that struck the crowd. In times of real trouble it is the real Jesus alone who can help, not some pretty picture of a trouble-free and attractive young hero.

Mark closes this section of the story by telling us how, as Jesus strode ahead, he was interrupted by a blind beggar. We can picture the whole procession coming to a stop. "Son of David, Jesus, have pity on me!" the voice rang out piteously, and the crowd told him to shut up. But Jesus stopped. And again his question: "What do you want me to do for you?" We are so accustomed to thinking of Jesus as a kind of automatic dispenser of healing of the body and soul that the question startles us. What else would blind man want but sight? Yet, as always, Jesus waits to be asked. There may be something he wants you to ask. This man needed the physical restoration of his sight. And I am sure that Mark includes his story here because he knew that every one of his readers needed the gift of inward vision. After all we learn from walking the Jerusalem Road with Jesus, who is not conscious of a need to see as Jesus saw, to have one's eyes opened to the reality of God's kingdom and the power of a life of self-giving love?

"Many scolded him and told him to be quiet." There

are plenty of forces in our world today that scold us for bothering about Jesus and his Church. "Forget it!" they say. "All this stuff about love and service and following Jesus is old hat. This is a world of grab and keep." But we need the lungs of Bartimaeus to call out: "I'm not impressed with your world of grab and keep. I want the way of Jesus. Son of David, have mercy on me!"

"What do you want me to do for you?" Jesus asked him. "Teacher," the blind man answered, "I want to see again." "Go," Jesus told him, "your faith has made you well."

Well, this is where the picture of Jesus on his way to Jerusalem has led us. If, in watching that picture you and I have walked even an inch or two with Jesus on the Jerusalem road, if as we have seen him in action and caught the echo of his words, and if one little window has opened for you into that kingdom where he reigns, then I would close by saying: "Go, your faith is making you well."

With the inward eye, O God, we would see Jesus as he was, as he is, and as he will be forever—the truly good, the compassionate, the pure in heart, the great giver of himself, the troubler of our conscience, and the restorer of our faith, our Lord and our Savior. Make us disciples who follow with more awe and obedience and much less fear, for his name's sake. Amen.

13

Through Hell with Jesus

Across the country today there is an atmosphere of uneasiness and apprehension, aroused by the stories of violence that we are constantly hearing. We can't open a newspaper or turn on the radio or television without being confronted by horrifying tales of murder, suicide, muggings, kidnappings, and brutalities of various kinds. I have no idea whether or not there is more violence and cruelty in the land today than there was in any other era, but we certainly hear more about it. There is no longer any quiet corner where peaceable people can live in comfortable ignorance of the horrors that may be happening elsewhere. The thought is now never very far away: "It could happen next door; it could happen here; it could happen to me."

More than ever we need a religion that reckons with a dangerous world and doesn't turn a blind eye to the vicious and violent streak in human nature. Faith has to mean something more than "looking on the bright side" and "hoping for the best." If there is to be a divine Lord in whom I put my trust it must be a Lord who knows what it is to be at the mercy of human violence and who can assure me that, in spite of the terrible things that human hate can do, there is a love that is stronger still. To put it another way, the one who speaks to me about heaven must know what it is to go through hell. And this is just what I find in the Gospel story. This is why the symbol of the Christian faith is a cross—not a pretty and bejewelled cross to decorate a shallow religion, but a plain reminder that the Son of God was the victim of the worst that we can do to one another.

Have you ever noticed that the account of the last week of the life of Jesus takes up nearly a third of the story in the Gospels? That was the week, known as Holy Week, when all the things we are afraid of seemed to take over: violence, hatred, bitterness, cruelty, and hardness of heart. This should remind us that these Gospels are not simple biographies of Jesus. They were written in the first place to tell people about the good news of Jesus and to nourish the faith of those early Christians who were threatened by a very hostile world. And they come to life for us again, as we listen to the story of Jesus and discover who he is and what he does for us. The Gospels were not written as a source book for scholars, but as a handbook for the faithful as they faced the onslaughts of the world, the flesh, and the devil, and sought to be loyal to their Lord. We find ourselves today in a similar situation. (Though our world is usually politely indifferent rather than actively hostile, our "flesh" is coddled by psychological excuses, and our devil wears a black tie.) We need exactly the same kind of encounter with the real Jesus, the Son of God who wins through the horrors to a Resurrection victory.

The Gospel writers seem to me to be saying something like this as they reach Holy Week: "We've told you the kind of person Jesus was; what he said, and what he did. Now let us tell you what they did to him during that last week in Jerusalem." They turn, as it were, from the action to the passion. And it is in the story of this passion that the first Christians found the heart of the good news. This has never been easy for the world to understand. What other religion has proposed to us a Savior who was insulted, attacked, betrayed, spat upon, tortured, and killed—not in some mythical drama or fanciful ritual, but in a world we know only too well, a world of intrigue, corruption, hatred, terrorism, and a balance of powers? It's never been easy even for Christians to understand, especially in times of relative comfort and security. Yet here is the story, and it may be that we are more ready to listen as our comforts and security wane. Here is the good news of a Lord who knows the worst that can happen to us, the extremes of human depravity and despair, and the full range of the powers of darkness that threaten the body and the soul. Remember that those who first heard this story knew that this Lord was alive, and every line of this tale was written by one who was in daily communion with the risen Christ. And it is of this living Jesus that we are told this terrible tale of the six days in Jerusalem when, quite literally, he went through hell for us.

"He descended into hell." I never hear or repeat these words of the Creed without thinking of what happened to Jesus from the moment of the ironic triumph of Palm Sunday to the last cry from the cross. Hell is one short word to cover the dark side of human experience—the pains of body and spirit, the sense of meaninglessness, isolation, and abandonment, the fear of the irrational and the demonic, and the abyss of nothingness where God himself seems to disappear. For me the compelling power of Christ lies in the fact that he has been *there*. He descended through every circle of that hell, and there is no blow he did not feel, no horror he did not stare upon, and no death he did not die. And he went through it all here where we live, and not in the pious imagination of some myth-spinning scribe.

How do we know it really happened? How do we know anything about what happened long ago? We can know only through the testimony of witnesses and our belief in their credibility. And I defy anyone to read these accounts and dismiss them as fiction. They are far too detailed, realistic, and even incomplete. It sounds exactly the way people remember any series of terrible and exciting events. This is how the disciples told the story of that week while groups of Christians like us listened.

Let's look at the incidents of that week and see how Jesus moved deeper and deeper into that region of loneliness, desolation, and pain to which we commonly give the name of hell. It begins with the tragic misunderstandings of the Palm Sunday parade. I want you to view it now as a symbol of the loneliness of Jesus, who alone knew what it meant to be the Messiah of God's design—the suffering servant on whom the Lord was laying "the iniquity of us all." The disciples beside Jesus still didn't understand. The cheering crowd with their shouts of "God bless the coming kingdom of our father David" have another kind of Messiah in mind. The scowling ecclesiastics see him as a false Messiah, a popular preacher with delusions of grandeur. The Romans, always nervous at festival times, see a native guru whose followers are likely to cause trouble. At this point Jesus must be going through the agony of isolation. Wherever he looks no one understands. I have never thought much of Jean-Paul Sartre's remark that "hell is other people." In the ultimate Christian sense, "heaven is other people." But here the total lack of true response must make it true for Jesus.

There are moments when all of us go through the hell of loneliness. "Nobody understands," we say. I am not talking about the kind of person who mopes through life complaining, "Nobody understands me," but of the inevitable moment when we have to accept that we are alone with the inner self that no one else can penetrate. Do we realize what it means to say that the God we worship has been there, that his Son knows this particular hell, and therefore is with us then as the One who understands?

In the succeeding days of Holy Week, as Jesus became embroiled in controversy, and witnessed the religious bigotry, political arrogance, popular cynicism and superstition, greed, lying, and brutality mix into a hell's brew that poisons everything he stood for, he wept over the city and its apparent surrender to the demonic powers he tried to exorcise. This is the hell that every sensitive man or woman passes through when the world we know and love turns

ugly, when we feel the ordinary decencies of life threatened by forces we didn't know were there, when we are
aware of the dark forces that surface through the veneer of
our civilization of law and order.

Some time ago, I read that when the mayor of a large
American city appointed five clergymen to investigate
charges of police corruption, a politician erupted in protest.
I quote from his remarks: "What the hell do they know
about crime? To them everyone is a good guy because that's
what the Lord says." Leaving aside the possibility that the
clergy, by nature of their work, learn a good deal about
crime and sin, I wonder what Bible this councilman was
using. For what my Lord says is that "from the inside, from
a man's heart, come the evil ideas which lead him to do
immoral things, to rob, kill, commit adultery, be greedy, and
do all sorts of evil things: deceit, indecency, jealousy, slan-
der, pride, and folly—all these evil things come from inside
a man" (Mark 7:20).

The point is that the more sensitive people are to the
Word of God and the claims of Christ, the more aware they
are of the powers of evil, and the more they suffer. If we
suffer in any way as we experience, or read about, the
corruptions of our society, think how Jesus suffered as these
forces ran amok in his Jerusalem. It was another circle of
his hell, and because he has been there, we need not fear
that any human society is totally at the mercy of these
demons. For this final passion of Jesus was his mightiest
exorcism, and the cross marked the worst his enemies
could do. As Paul once wrote, "Having drawn the sting of
all the powers ranged against us, he exposed them, shat-
tered, empty and defeated, in his final, glorious triumphant
act!" (Col. 2:15).

Then, as that week moved inexorably to Good Friday,
he knew the hell of betrayal, when even his closest friends
deserted, of fear as the reality of the suffering closed in on
him in the Garden of Gethsemane, and then of the frightful
physical pain of his torture and death. Let no one brush all
this aside with the thought that for a saint these things are

nothing compared with mental suffering and spiritual desolation. While Mark's story contains no loaded words to
arouse our emotions, his blunt, factual statements are all the
more shattering. He makes it plain that Jesus shrank, as we
would, from the agony of the scourging, the nailing, and the
slow death upon the cross. Such pain is hell—and Jesus
went through it. He knows what it is. Our God knows what
it is, though he hasn't explained it, at least not to my
satisfaction. But in his Son he has endured it, and in our
pain we need never be alone.

"He descended into hell." We now come to the last
literal meaning of that word. For ultimately hell is to be
without God. Its shadows are the sense of utter emptiness in
a universe without meaning. It's when nothing seems to
matter anymore, and there is no one on earth or in heaven
who cares. It is reflected in the current literature of despair
and the absurd, but has found a voice in the Psalms, in Job,
in Aeschylus, in Shakespeare, and wherever the spirit of
man has confronted the abyss. What matters most is that
few go through life without some journey through this darkness, and when it happens we think we are alone. We are
not. Others have been there. Others are there now. And
Mark tells us in words that some would tear out of the
Gospel record that Jesus was there too.

"At three o'clock Jesus cried out with a loud shout,
'Eloi, Eloi, lema sabachthani?' which means, "My God, my
God, why did you abandon me?' " This was hell indeed.
Where else could he go if he were to experience the last
possible agony of our human condition, and if he were
indeed bearing the full burden of our fears and sins? There
was no more he could do, no more he could suffer. It was
finished. "With a loud cry Jesus died" (Mark 15:34).

We might now ask if this story of the passion is simply
the unrelieved description of how the Son of God went
through hell for us. Are there no signs that someone understood? Are all human beings in this story either criminals,
bigots, tyrants, or cowards? By no means. I think of the
children shouting in the temple, and of the scribe who

agreed with Jesus that loving God and our fellow men was more important than offering animal sacrifices on the altar, and was told "you are not far from the kingdom of God." I think also of the poor widow who acted out her love by dropping two tiny coins in the box at the temple, of whom Jesus said, "I tell you that this poor widow put more in the offering box than all the others." But above all I think of the soldier on duty at the foot of the cross. "The army officer," writes Mark, "who was standing there at the front of the cross, saw how Jesus had cried out and died. 'This man was really the Son of God,' " he said (Mark 15:39).

I hear him speaking for the ordinary man or woman of any period in history, when confronted by Jesus, who has gone through hell. So often people say: "I'm not religious and don't know the right way to express what I feel about Jesus," or "I'm no theologian and don't know what you mean by Son of God." Do you suppose this soldier was particularly religious in our sense of the word? Do you imagine that he really knew what he was saying? Luke says that he simply said: "Surely this man was innocent." What does it matter? Somehow he was moved by what he saw, he responded, and he knew that what was going on affected him. It was his hand of faith going out, like the hand of a child in the darkness, and I believe that in the mystery of heaven it was caught and held.

No two of us respond in exactly the same way to the story of the Passion. There is no one formula by which we acknowledge this suffering, yet triumphant, Son of God. But we know our need, and we glimpse a Savior who can meet that need, the One who went through hell to be with us in our suffering, the One who went through hell for us so that we shall never be there to stay. "For I am persuaded that neither death, nor life, nor angels, nor principalities, nor powers, nor things present, nor things to come, nor height, nor depth, nor any other creature, shall be able to separate us from the love of God, which is in Christ Jesus our Lord" (Rom. 8:38,39).

Father-God we confess that sometimes we give way to fear when we feel the violence and cruelties that threaten our world. Help us so to see Jesus as he went from Gethsemane to Calvary, and from Calvary to Easter morning, that we may find in him the Savior we need and the giver of thy peace and joy; for his sake. Amen.

14

Unfinished Easter

The greatest joy for one who is called to minister in the name of Christ is to rise in the pulpit on Easter day and greet the congregation with the thrilling and ancient salutation: Christ is risen! For the Resurrection is at the center of all that I believe.

Like Paul I feel that "if Christ be not risen, then is our preaching in vain, and your faith is also vain." That Jesus not only came back from the dead, and that he is still alive is the one miracle that really matters. Therefore, I rejoice in repeating with the entire Church in every age and in every land: "The third day he rose again from the dead."

But now I want to draw your attention to a rather strange fact—that the Gospels give us very brief and sober accounts of the Resurrection. You read nowhere of a majestic rending of the tomb, radiant disciples, and angel songs. There is nothing in these books that resembles the medieval paintings that show Jesus emerging from the tomb and confounding his enemies by his risen splendor. Indeed, if you read through the Gospel of Mark in a modern version you will experience a sense of disappointment, almost anticlimax, at the very end of the book.

After the Sabbath day was over, Mary Magdalene, Mary the mother of James, and Salome brought spices to go and anoint the body of Jesus. Very early on Sunday morning, at sunrise, they went to the grave. On the way they said to one another, "Who will roll away the stone from the entrance to the grave for us?" (It was a very large stone.) Then they looked up and saw that the stone had already been rolled back. So they entered the grave, where they saw a young man, sitting at the right, who wore a white robe—and they were filled with alarm. "Don't be alarmed," he said. "You are looking for Jesus of Nazareth, who was nailed to the cross. But he is not here—he has risen! Look, here is the place where they laid him. Now go and give this message to his disciples, including Peter: 'He is going to Galilee ahead of you; there you will see him, just as he told you.' " So they went out and ran from the grave, because fear and terror were upon them. And they said nothing to anyone, because they were afraid (Mark 16:1-8).

This is how the story ends according to the oldest manuscripts. After the thrills of the Gallilean campaign, the mounting tensions of Holy Week, and the horrendous climax of the crucifixion, Mark's story of the Resurrection does seem rather a letdown. Wouldn't you expect at least one glittering chapter to round off the story, with the crucified Jesus seen again by all his disciples, alive and triumphant? This section reads more like a postscript than a climax. It's as if Mark were saying: "This is Jesus, who brought good news to us all, the Son of God who taught and healed and cast out demons, the Son of man who went through hell for us and was finally crucified, dead and buried. P.S. They found his tomb empty on the third day."

The final words, as Mark wrote them, are the most puzzling and unexpected of all. Instead of ending with a dramatic encounter with the risen Christ and a chorus of hallelujahs, he tells us that the women who found the tomb empty "said nothing to anyone, because they were afraid." Yes, these are the words with which this earliest Gospel ends: *ephobounto gar*, "for they were afraid."

I needn't tell you that the scholars, faced with a literary puzzle like this, have for centuries produced theory after theory to account for the abrupt ending of Mark's gospel. The manuscript was torn and the real ending lost. It was meant to be followed immediately by Resurrection stories from Matthew and Luke. Some skeptic actually excised Resurrection stories he didn't believe in. All these things have happened to ancient manuscripts and are perfectly possible. Others tell a dramatic tale of Mark writing in prison and being interrupted at this point by a guard tapping him on the shoulder and saying, "Come." That too is possible. I know, because it once happened to me when I was writing a lecture in a prison camp; I still have the manuscript, broken off in midsentence.

But you were not invited on Easter Day for an exercise in textual criticism. Let me tell you why I believe that this is exactly how Mark left his Gospel, and how this deliberately unfinished Easter story can today be for us the strongest challenge to our faith. It is just because the story is left hanging that it draws us into the picture. A rounded-off, completed story of Jesus might be something we could admire and hold at a distance, but this open-ended Gospel stretches out to this year of grace. It suggests a meeting with Jesus that can take place now. It is an invitation to you and me to write our own endings. And that is exactly what happens when a man or woman today in New York, St. Louis, Seattle, or any other place makes the discovery that Jesus is alive.

I accept the ending as it is because it is in the style of Mark. He never dramatizes. He gives us the facts. Without any attempt at eloquence or artistry he tells what happened. He names the women who saw the body of Jesus placed in the tomb, and tells us that when they returned after the Sabbath for the anointing, the body was no longer there. A mysterious young man then told the women that Jesus had been raised from the dead and would meet his disciples in Galilee. That's all he says except to add that the

women were terrified. That may be a curious way to end
his Gospel—"they were afraid"—but it certainly has the
ring of truth. We're so used to thinking of the joy of the
disciples when they knew that Jesus was alive again that
we forget how terrifying the first news of such a miracle
must have been. Honestly, if you were told that a friend
you had seen dead and buried was walking around alive
again wouldn't you be scared out of your wits?

So Mark delivers the news, calmly and realistically,
leaving others to draw their conclusions. The tomb was
empty. There is enormous power in his laconic statement of
fact. The dead body of Jesus represented the defeat of all
he stood for and the triumph of his enemies. We should
have to say that the demonic forces of hatred, corruption,
violence, and death had the last word. The world had chosen Barabbas and the world was right. There is no stronger
power than the evil we know, and the blood-stained body
of Jesus disintegrates leaving the memory of a brief, glorious, but ultimately futile life. But the Church of Christ was
not built upon the corpse of a martyr. Behind Mark's laconic account we hear the word of the living God who had
raised his Son from the dead and set him loose in the
world until the day of his final triumph.

Mark doesn't bother to tell us that Mary Magdalene
met the risen Jesus, that Peter met him, and James and John
and Thomas. For he knows that others met him and will go
on meeting him through the centuries. The man who told of
the empty tomb and the terror of the women had himself
met the living Christ or he would never have written this
book. Again and again he had heard his friend Paul tell
how he had met Jesus on the Damascus road until Mark
must have nudged his neighbor and whispered: "Here it
comes again." He left the story unfinished because it can
never be finished until "every tongue confess that Jesus
Christ is Lord, to the glory of God the Father."

Therefore, I want to give you as an Easter text not one
of the New Testament statements about what happened on
Easter morning, but the words of another witness to the

living Christ, one who like Solzhenitsyn in our day, was banished from home for the sake of his convictions. Through him the Easter call comes, not as a reminder of something that happened long ago, but as a contemporary challenge, a living experience, a transforming presence of the divine. "Listen! I stand at the door and knock" (Rev. 3:20).

If anyone asks why this very religious generation is not battering at the doors of the churches instead of wandering through the corridors of the occult, gathering in charismatic groups, or taking the mystic road to Katmandu, my answer would be that, on the whole, we have failed to present the Gospel as a living experience. We have become reporters of the religious experience. We have become reporters of the religious experience of others from Abraham to Bonhoeffer, rather than catalysts of the living Christ. Instead of bringing people into vital contact with him, and conveying the excitement of life in the Spirit, we have tended to offer what I might call an A.B.C. of theology and an N.B.C. of current affairs. We are suffering from the blight of the second-hand—honoring someone else's God, interested in someone else's Jesus, keeping the Gospel at one remove from the center of our lives. So Easter may become nothing more than an exercise in religious nostalgia to the sound of trumpets.

"Listen! I stand at the door and knock." I like this translation better than the conventional, "Behold!" You don't watch someone knocking on the other side of the door; you hear him. The words of Jesus—all of them, not just the ones we cull out for our comfort—have been knocking on the doors of prejudice, laziness, self-indulgence, and moral defeat that we keep closed against him. We have heard that knocking as we watch him at work caring, healing, forgiving, and casting out devils. It grows louder as we see what happened in Jerusalem when he drew unto himself the curse of our mixed-up world, and died for the sins we recognize in society and in our hearts. Now on this Easter Day I hear a crescendo of knocks as this same Jesus asks to be admitted to cleanse the inner temple of our lives, and to bring life and victory to the very places where there have been death and defeat. "If anyone hears my voice and opens the door, I will come into his house and eat with him, and he will eat with me" (Rev. 3:20). With song and prayer, surrounded by his worshipping Church on earth and in heaven, we say, "Even so, come, Lord Jesus."

It was a loud knocking they heard in the Church of Laodicea when the letter was first read. It was a loud knocking that Saul of Tarsus heard on the Damascus road. And it is a loud knocking that many of us have heard at moments of intense emotion when the realm of the spirit suddenly becomes close—a birth, a death, a sudden danger, or an overwhelming joy. It may be so loud for someone listening today that at last you want to write your own ending to the Easter story and invite the living Jesus to come in. "If anyone hears my voice and opens the door"— the latch is on the inside and you can use it now—"I will come in." He doesn't say he will bring the heavenly orchestra with him to flood your soul with music. He may, but what he promises is just that intimate communion that you have with a good friend over a common meal. "I will eat with him and he will eat with me." And that's what we need for the daily road.

But the knocking is seldom loud. In fact, these days it often seems to be so quiet we can hardly hear it. Our noisy world has drowned it out. It is perfectly possible for a man or woman to be so deafened by the traffic of the secular world that this knock from beyond cannot be heard. Yet even with the din there is a gentle knocking that an increasing number seem to be hearing. The first-hand religious experience I have talked about is not something that can come only in the quiet, or I should have to give you Hamlet's advice to Ophelia: "Get thee to a nunnery!" There is a gentle knocking in our society warning us that all is not well, and it penetrates our confusion. Whenever we feel disquiet with the kind of life that is promised by our materialist age; whenever we feel sickened by the philosophy of "anything goes"; whenever we feel an urge to take a stand for things like honesty, decency, truth, beauty, reverence, and compassion—Jesus is knocking at the door.

A church should be a place where we can hear that knock. Of course, the living Christ is abroad in this world and not locked up in these sanctuaries. But to be in church is to give ourselves a chance to hear his voice. To be a church member should be to get to know others who have this same desire. To confess Christ in the community of his church is one way of opening that door. Every Sunday is for the true Christian an Easter Day.

So Mark didn't finish the Easter story. No, he left you to write your own. The living Christ is here in what some call the Age of Melancholy to walk into every corner of your life bringing his compassion, his vitality, his hope, and his joy. Will you open the door?

Today, O Father, we turn from all frustration, folly, and defeat to rejoice with the whole Church in the victory of Jesus Christ our Lord. Grant us grace, whatever our circumstances, to lift the latch and welcome the Savior; to add to the chorus our own hallelujah! Amen.

15

Living by the Energy of God

Not long ago we all became aware of something called an energy crisis. It had to do with a sudden shortage of the power that drives our cars, heats our homes, and keeps the factories going. An energy crisis means that not enough is coming through. We have been forced to think about the energy on which modern society depends, and which we had been taking for granted. We have learned that gas is not always just automatically in the pumps, or electricity always flowing to our homes. The trouble is not that there are not enough sources of energy in our part of the world. We have water, wind, sun, coal, oil, and nuclear power, but these sources are not being developed quickly enough, and the channels of distribution have been clogged. The supply is there, but its use has been limited not so much by lack of technical knowledge, as by human folly and fear. Not only have affluent societies squandered energy, but fear has led the great powers to expend huge quantities on weapons of destruction.

It's part of my Christian belief that the ultimate source of all energy is God. It is among the gifts of the creator to his human family. When the psalmist sings: "All thy works praise thee, O God," and exults that the human race has been made "to have dominion over all the works of thy hands," *works* means energy. So when Jesus said: "My Father has never ceased his work," he was speaking of the divine energy still pulsing in our world. To believe in God the Creator means for me that his energy is the source of all the power we have needed from the day that fire was first discovered to the complex requirements of modern society. What we do with this energy that God has provided is our decision. We can squander it; we can blow ourselves up with it; or we can follow the Bible's instructions and be good stewards of God's gift, using energy with reverence and compassion.

But it's another kind of energy that I am chiefly concerned with now. Most of us had energy crises long before we lined up for gasoline or turned down the thermostat. I'm thinking of the psychic energy that ebbs and flows within us—the inner power that makes us say that one person is energetic and another not. And we all know how this energy supply varies from day to day, even from hour to hour. Sometimes we seem to be swept along by some inner fuel that helps us get things done and inspires us to look for new tasks. We enjoy meeting people. Ideas bubble up in our minds. What we believe as Christians comes to life, enabling us to respond to the grace of God, and delight in unexpected joys, cope with unexpected troubles, and look ahead with high hopes and expectations. At other times our energy seems to have drained away overnight. We wake up wondering how ever we are going to get through the tasks of the day, and we go listlessly about our jobs, not very enthusiastic about meeting anybody, and with nothing but tired old ideas circulating in our heads. At such times, we are prime targets for commercials about anemia or tired blood. And what we believe as Christians seems rather dim and distant. It is as if our energy were tucked away in some far corner of the mind rather than energizing the body, mind, and spirit and sending us singing on our way. There may be some people in whom the energy flows steadily and unceasingly, but I am not one of them—and neither, I suspect, are you.

There are probably a hundred and one reasons for this occasional lack of energy, but I find it helpful to think of the parallel with the material energy crisis. For I have come to believe more strongly than ever that God is the source of this psychic energy as well as providing the fuel for our material needs. So, using the same reasoning, the energy is there, and nine times out of ten the reason for our lassitude is that the channels of communication have been clogged. This idea of God as the source of energy is, I find, not hard for most people to accept. Indeed many will say that this is the only kind of God they can believe in—the mysterious power which is beyond the human but need not be called divine. Some, in fact, would simply say that energy is God, including in that concept the thought that God is also the psychic energy that moves in the spirit of man. Since nowadays it is increasingly difficult to make clear distinctions between matter and spirit, we are left with the thought that we are beneficiaries, or the victims, of a vast cosmic energy that beats in the heart of the universe.

Now let me tell you why I don't find such thinking sufficient as a working faith. For one thing it tells me nothing about the moral life. We are left ignorant about how to choose between good and evil, right and wrong. We know that physical energy can be used both for the benefit of mankind and for its destruction. We are learning that psychic energy can be similarly creative or destructive. Not all psychic energy is good. The energy that invaded Hitler and Stalin was enormous, and we know what they became and for what they were responsible. I was once within a few yards of Adolf Hitler and sensed something of what could only be called demonic energy—enough to make me revise my rationalizing of what the New Testament calls "demon-possession." If I'm going to talk of cosmic psychic energy, I want to know what kind of energy it is, and whether or not such a God cares at all about good and evil.

This is where the Gospel leaps to life for me. What the Bible declares and what comes to focus in the person of Jesus Christ is the reality of a divine energy of love. Since love is not an abstract quality found in the earth, the oceans, or outer space, but intensely human, personal activity, I am gripped by the Bible's revelation of a personal God. It's strange to me that many stumble at this point, as if this meant conceiving of God as a kind of superman located somewhere in space. Both Christians and Jews are unashamed to believe in a God who reflects in perfection the highest that we know—goodness, wisdom, beauty, and, supremely, love. Since we grasp love through personal experience or through a story, rather than by abstract definition, I rejoice in the story of God's love made visible in Christ and alive by his spirit. The energy of God is an energy of love—that for me is the meaning of the story that runs from Bethlehem to Calvary. This energy is still powerful today; that's the meaning of Easter and Pentecost.

This is a good time to think about the question of our flagging moral energy. Recent events have led many people to worry about our ethical standards, and the need for dynamic leadership to overcome what sometimes seems like a paralysis of the soul. My own belief is that such leadership in every aspect of our national life depends on a renewal of faith in the energy of God. This is beautifully expressed in a verse of Scripture that is often used at the end of sermons as an ascription of praise. It may be familiar to you, but I wonder if you have caught its inner meaning. The words are: "Now unto him that is able to do exceedingly abundantly above all that we ask or think, according to the power that worketh in us, unto him be glory in the church by Christ Jesus throughout all ages, world without end. Amen" (Eph. 3:20,21). For many the cadence of these words indicates that the sermon is over, that the preacher is signing off. Any text ending with the words "world without end" is apt to float over our heads as conventional ecclesiastical noise. But at the heart of this text is a phrase that summarizes all I believe about the

energy of God, and throbs with the good news of the
Gospel.

"According to the power that worketh in us. . . ." The
apostle is talking to people like us, struggling to live by the
Gospel and terribly conscious of their deficiency in spiritual
energy and moral power. And he goes right to the point
when he speaks of "the power that worketh in us. . . ." He's
telling us that there really is a God who cares about the
kind of people we are, and who can supply the spiritual
dynamic that we need. He's not a God who simply says:
"There's the right way, now get on with it," but one who
supplies the power that we need. I was excited to discover
that the Greek words Paul used here were those from
which we get our words *dynamic* and *energy*. The literal
translation of this phrase is "by the dynamic that energizes
us." The word *energy* simply means "working within," so
Christian life is described as living by the energy of God.

Sometimes when ministers meet and compare notes
about their congregations, statistics of membership are apt
to be thrown around. Then someone will usually say: "Now
honestly how many *live* members have you got?" We all
know what's meant, although few of us like to set ourselves
up as judge and jury concerning other peoples' faith, or
lack of it. The fact is that in any congregation some people
respond more actively than others. I'm not thinking so
much about response to the programs and appeals of the
church, as response to the Gospel—the signs that a man or
woman is taking the affirmation "Jesus Christ is my Lord
and Savior" seriously, and that the fruit of the spirit is to be
seen in their lives. Wherever I have worked as a pastor I
have found these live Christians, have thanked God for
them, and have learned from them. I have also, thank God,
seen others come alive. Call it conversion, or what you will,
seeing this does more to reinforce my own faith in Christ
than a library of apologetics. These alive Christians are not
necessarily very busy about what we call "church work,"
and they are certainly not aggressively religious or proud of
their moral attainments. They are people of every age and

every walk of life, who somehow have come to know the
secret of living by the energy of God.

This is an open secret, you know. It means realizing
that of all the influences that surround us in our daily life
potentially the greatest is the grace of God. It means keeping open the channels of communication by prayer, worship, and constant reference to his will. It means knowing
that the power of God is energizing us, even on days when
we feel dull and unresponsive. It means living with the
conviction that God is able to do for us "above all that we
ask or think. . . ." There is no standard model for the Christian life, no book of rules that applies to everybody. Being a
Christian is being your true self, the self that is energized
by the dynamic that works within you, the energy of God.

This text can also be translated "according to the power that is at work among us," offering another insight into
Christian life. None of us is a pure individual. We can't
live by the energy of God without reference to the community of Christians. The energy of God is mediated to us
many times by the community of the Church, beginning
with that little church which was our parents. We are dis-
covering today, perhaps in a new way, how dependent we
are on one another. Our experience of the energy of God is
sustained by the energy of the Christian community,
through worship in our local churches or in groups where
faith is shared and burdens unloaded.

The "power that worketh in us" and among us, is, of
course, another name for the Holy Spirit. We hear more
about the Holy Spirit these days precisely because more are
seeking the energy that works inside each Christian and
binds us together as a real community of faith. Everything
today that breaks down barriers between people, loosens
Christians up to be more open with one another and with
God, and creates a kind of fellowship that is real and deep,
helps the energy of God to flow more powerfully in each of
us.

We are well beyond the days when a minimal amount
of Christianity was assumed to be normal and there was no

clear line between belief and unbelief. Now it is plain that either we believe that there is such a thing as the energy of God, or we don't; that we have discovered this to be an energy of love, or we haven't; and that we are committed to living by the spirit of Christ within us and among us, or we aren't. I believe that this spirit is calling everyone to begin again, living by the energy of God. So let me end with the ascription that carries this message to each one of us: "Now unto him that is able to do exceedingly abundantly above all that we ask or think, according to the power that worketh in us, unto him be glory in the Church by Christ Jesus throughout all ages [including ours], world without end. Amen."

We thank thee, O God, that thou hast promised that those who wait on thee shall renew their strength, mount up with wings as eagles, run and not be weary, walk and not faint. Make us surer than ever of the indwelling power of thy Spirit, and enable us to live as those who derive their energy from thee and are open channels for thy love; through Jesus Christ our Lord. Amen.

16

The Motherhood of God

I remember once being asked a question by an agnostic friend, which I found exceedingly difficult to answer. It was: "What do you actually think about when you say *God?*" It's a perfectly fair question but it's not easy to describe what kind of image comes to mind when I use this word. We seldom think much about our image of God. Most of us have been taught something about him as infants, and we grow up using the name *God,* and surrounding it with mental pictures we don't really care to examine. It's often assumed that all Christians have more or less the same picture of God in their minds, and that when a congregation is invited to pray we all are thinking about the same being and have an identical image hovering around us. If that were ever true, it's certainly not true today. If we could at this moment share with one another our private conceptions of God I'm sure we'd find a huge variety, ranging from the most vague and impersonal to the most vivid and anthropomorphic.

Perhaps you feel that it would be better not to raise the question at all. I find there are many people who would rather not examine basic religious questions of this kind. They are afraid of losing something precious if they disturb

the assumptions with which they have been living happily
for years. Their motto is: "Let sleeping gods lie." I agree that
we shouldn't forever be ferreting around to discover what
we really believe. But it's a timid kind of faith that fears
bringing such questions to the light of day, and every now
and then it's good for us to be challenged concerning our
ideas of the God to whom we pray. At least anyone who
offers to talk about his own faith must be willing to talk
about this.

I found myself so challenged just the other day. Ministers are expected to talk about God and to be ready with a
prayer at the drop of a hat—meaning they are exceptionally
vulnerable to what might be called automatic or thoughtless
prayer. If you are accustomed to using certain prayers regularly in public, for instance at weddings and funerals, you
have to be alert not to let the words slip out without thought
about the God to whom we pray. I've learned that nothing
is so challenging as saying prayers aloud in the presence of
a skeptical five-year-old. And it is devastating, after such a
prayer, to be met with the open-eyed question: "God isn't
real, is he, Daddy?" Bang go all one's assumptions about
the natural piety of children. Admittedly, this particular
child was at the stage of sorting out the "real," such as his
school friends, from the "unreal," by which he means the
assorted characters from our private mythology about whom
we make up absurd stories. But it was good for me to face
the question about how real God has been to me as I
prayed that night. What a difference there is between prayers that trip off the tongue, and those moments when the
reality of God overwhelms us and we know he is the reality
before whom everything else pales, the one refuge and
strength for all our thinking and living.

I was reminded then of the testimony of an English
officer, who claimed to be an agnostic, to the faith of Die-
trich Bonhoeffer, the young German theologian with whom
he shared those last days before Bonhoeffer was hanged by
the Nazis. He had heard from him no conventional prayers
or pious cliche's, yet this is what he wrote: "Bonhoeffer was

all humility and sweetness, he always seemed to diffuse an
atmosphere of happiness, of joy in the smallest events in
life, and of deep gratitude for the mere fact that he was
alive. . . . He was one of the very few men I have ever met
to whom his God was real and close to him."[1] Yet Bonhoeffer was one of those who dared to question his image
of God and to open up all kinds of new thoughts about our
deepest beliefs.

I believe that God is real, yet all of us know moments
when his reality is less than compelling. Don't we sometimes offer prayers without really stopping to think about
the one to whom they are addressed? Who is he? How shall
we think or speak about him? Or should I be saying *he* and
him at all?

I find it comforting that the Bible sets up warning
signals against any attempt to define God or to portray him
with any physical or mental images. The condemnation of
idolatry means that no image, either in stone or in the mind,
can be declared to be God himself. Thus, there is room for
a great variety of thoughts and pictures when we think of
God—provided we don't ever say: "This is it; here in a
package is the God in whom you must believe." It's strange
how many still think that this is what we do in church—
that we have a standard definition of God to which all must
subscribe. Just because God is God he cannot be bounded
by any limitations imposed by human hands or human
minds. We all recognize the absurdity of thinking, as Paul
once pointed out to the Athenians, "that the Godhead is like
unto gold, or silver, or stone, graven by art and man's
device." But do we also recognize the absurdity of thinking
that God can be finally described by the language of our
creeds?

The Bible brings us a living God, a God who acts and
is not just a beautiful and logical idea. We get to know God
by what he has done, what he is doing, and what he will

---

[1]Dietrich, Bonhoeffer, *Letters & Papers from Prison* (New York: Macmillan
Co., 1972), p 11.

do. When he is called Creator, we're not sticking a label on some mental image that might mean little or nothing. We are being exposed to the Bible picture of the spirit of God breathing life into the primeval chaos. We are hearing the music of creation "when the morning stars sang together, and all the sons of God shouted for joy." When we say that God is love we are not just adding one abstraction to another. We are acknowledging the yearning, inexhaustible, motherlike, love of God for his human family. We are being told that this God "so loved the world that he gave his only Son." We are being touched at the center of our beings by a living Lord who is not only real but near: "closer is he than breathing, nearer than hands or feet." What keeps many from a lively faith in God may well be a tendency to think with nouns rather than with verbs, things rather than actions. The Hebrew genius of the Bible throws the emphasis on the verbs: God is what he does.

To describe what he does the Bible deals not only in the stories of his mighty acts, but in metaphors, similes, parables, and poetry. These naturally reflect the life and times of the writers. In days when monarchy was the keystone of the political order, it was natural for God's sovereignty to be expressed in terms of royalty and kingship. In an agricultural economy, it was inevitable that the prophetic imagery for God's tender care and concern should be drawn from the shepherd and his flock. And in a patriarchal society where the father-figure was dominant, thoughts about God's relationship to his people would circle around the thought of the Father. In the Old Testament this figure is sparingly used: it was left to Jesus to risk the thought that the best of all names for God in his day would be the unpatriarchal diminutive Abba, "Daddy."

I feel that it's important that none of these metaphors should be allowed to freeze our picture of God, as if all had been said once we use a particular word. We're always in danger of fastening on God the prejudices and limitations of our own society and our own experiences. What about this word Father? It conveyed one thing to an an-

cient tribesman whose father was a fearful figure with powers of life and death; something else to the friends of Jesus
whose fathers were the kindly providers; and something
else again to the Victorians, whose fathers frown on us
from gilt-framed paintings. And it must mean something
else again to a generation raised on the image of the incom-
petent bumbling clown portrayed in so many soap operas.
In particular, we today must realize how subtly we have
transferred to our thoughts about God the masculine prejudices and assumptions that cluster round our use of male
language and imagery in the Christian Church.

This is why I am speaking to you today about the
motherhood of God. It's time we freed ourselves from the
tyranny of conventional language and faced the fact that, if
God is really God, then his qualities and actions cannot be
spoken of exclusively in male terms. The idea of father-
hood can suggest some deep and true thoughts about him—
but so can motherhood. It could be enriching to think about
some divine qualities that can best be described in terms of
the motherhood of God.

One is creativity. We all have this in common; we all
had a mother. So we all know what it is to have been given
life, as well as the unique ties that exist between every man
and woman and the mother. We can surely understand
how many primitive religions expressed the thought of creation in terms of a mother-goddess from whose womb everything comes. But when the God of the Bible was revealed and the pantheon of gods and goddesses gave way
to the stern monotheism of the Old Testament, this was not
some kind of sexist revolution that dethroned the female
deities and set up a supreme masculine figure as the Lord
of the universe. The point of this dynamic monotheism—
"thou shalt have no other gods"—was that in God Almighty
are all the qualities that we recognize in humanity at its
best, male and female, and that the universe is in the hands
of one good and infinitely trustworthy, Lord. Hence God
may surely be thought of not only as the "Great Father of

Glory, Pure Father of Light," as the hymn says, but also as
the Creative Mother from whom all creation comes.

If that sounds shocking to our ears we should listen
again to the Bible. For, in spite of the tendency of the
writers in both Old and New Testaments to draw on masculine imagery and metaphor, there are signs that the motherhood of God was also in their minds. The Holy Spirit is
often associated with the birth pangs of creation. Paul
speaks of "the whole created universe groaning in all its
parts as if with the pangs of childbirth." We are invited to
believe in a God who not only gives birth to all that is, but
through whom the miracle of rebirth also takes place. Jesus,
in his conversation with Nicodemus, links the thought of
natural birth ("Can he enter the second time into his mother's womb and be born?") with the inner awakening,
through which the Spirit gives new life to the sons and
daughters of God. This is why the Church that embodies
the Gospel of the rebirth is often spoken of as she, and why
Calvin, for instance, could say that no one is truly a Christian unless born in her womb and nourished at her breasts.
God is not only the Mother who has given birth to the
universe, but also the Mother who brings to birth the inner
life in which we awaken to the joys and duties of a living
faith.

Can we know that this living God cares for us as
deeply and truly as one human being can care for another?
It's not hard to believe in some kind of Creator-Spirit behind and within this mysterious universe. But we are faced
with the agonies and cruelties that lie in wait for even the
most fortunate of us, and immensities of space of which
Pascal said, "The eternal silence of infinite space terrifies
me." It may be difficult to believe that this Creator-Spirit
cares for each of us and wills our good. The Bible voices
this doubt but gives a bold and decisive answer. God cares
more than we can imagine. When one of the prophets
wanted to ransack all human experience to find the most
powerful example of human care that can possibly be con-

ceived, it was motherhood that came to mind. "Can a woman forget the child at her breast," he wrote, "or a loving mother the child of her womb?" Nowhere in all creation is there such caring as that of the mother for her child. Yet, says the prophet, it is conceivable that one could find a mother who ceased to care. "Yea, she may forget" is the word the prophet hears, "yet will I not forget thee."

What a word of God for us to hear! The holiest, highest, most enduring love that human nature can know is still flawed compared with the endless and overwhelming love of the Lord our God. That's not always easy to believe. In every age the cry has gone up that God has forgotten us, and probably no one has been exempt from the feeling that God doesn't really care. Yet this mother-love of God enshrines the unshakable promise that no matter what happens to us in life and death, he cares and goes on caring in that eternal world into which we go. Jesus lived his human life in the unswerving belief that nothing whatever can make God stop caring for his children, even when he allows them the freedom to curse, to lie, to enslave, and to make crosses on which to murder one another. Jesus' final words on his cross, "Father into thy hands I commend my spirit," expressed his belief that the ruler of all things is just and good. He might well have said, "Mother into thy hands I commend my spirit," for he believed that in the heart of the eternal is the strongest love it is given us to know.

Didn't most of us get our first inkling of what it means to have trust in the love of God from our own mothers? For our infant confidence in her was a foreshadowing of what it means to believe in God. We could not, and we cannot, believe that she would never cease to care. There may be troubles, quarrels, misunderstandings, but we know that the umbilical cord, cut at birth, can never be finally severed in the soul. The Bible message is that, strong though this tie may be, it is no more than a dim reflection of the immense caring of God. That is why, when we think of the God to whom we pray, his motherhood is more than a fancy; it is very real and very near.

O God we find it hard to understand that thy love for us surpasses anything we know on earth; yet this is the word of those who know thee best. So we once more confide our lives and those who are dear to us into thy care and protection in the name of Jesus Christ thy Son our Lord. Amen.

17

With Firm Faith and Wide Horizons

We're living in exciting times for religious beliefs. Nobody really knows what's happening. On the one hand there is evidence that the churches today are less well attended and supported than they were in the nineteen-fifties. On the other hand there is a wave of religious enthusiasm sweeping over sections of the community and a proliferation of cults, new and old, offering spiritual experiences of all kinds—from the loftiest to the sinister and alarming. The fifties were, on the whole, a period of conventional religious boom with great expansion of church life, church buildings, and church attendance. But it was not a time of spiritual excitement; nor was there much depth to the movement into the churches. So it was not surprising that when the sixties burst upon us the religious boom began to look more like a religious bust, with declining attendance, widespread questioning of traditional beliefs, and a massive exodus from the traditional patterns of church life. The watchword was *action*. To the consternation of the more conservative, churches launched out into social and political activities, protests, and demonstrations, while old forms of worship were discarded in favor of liturgical experiments, complete with banners, balloons, and dancing in the aisles. But once again there seemed to be little emphasis on the mystery of the faith, on profound personal religious experience, or on a sense of wonder and ecstasy.

Now, in the seventies, a new kind of religious explosion is going on. This time the accent is on the immediate, the transforming, as well as on the eternal dimension. There is no sign of a return to the conventional churchgoing of the fifties; and the activist wave of the sixties has receded. What, then, is happening? It's anybody's guess, but few can deny that there is a stirring of the Spirit in the land. The younger generation is in pursuit of lively and liberating religious experience from whatever direction it may come, and the most vigorous churches are those that proclaim an unashamedly supernatural Gospel and offer an experience of community in which lives are transformed. Barriers between denominations are being broken down, but not at all the way that was planned by the ecumenical enthusiasts of past decades. Today there is little interest in structures, organizations, and plans to bring different churches under some big ecclesiastical umbrella. But strange things are happening as Christians find themselves sharing in the empowering experience of the Holy Spirit, a new discovery of the Bible, or enterprises to minister to the afflicted and oppressed.

It may be that out of all this will come new life for the churches. It may also be that they are in for a period of attrition—if the spiritual quest of the seventies bypasses the old church-on-the-corner and spawns new forms of belief and new patterns of worship and devotion. A lot will depend on whether they nourish congregations with strong roots in the historic faith and an openness to the movement of the spirit in our day, or whether they are content simply to be religious clubs for those who like to flavor their lives with a sprinkling of conventional religion.

This leads me to a personal confession of what I believe is most needed at this critical period in Church history. It is best expressed in a prayer that you will find in the third chapter of the Epistle to the Ephesians. It is a prayer for any of us who professes any kind of allegiance to Jesus Christ. "With deep roots and firm foundations, may you be strong to grasp, with all God's people, what is the breadth and length and height and depth of the love of Christ, and to know it, though it is beyond knowledge" (Eph. 3:17-19).

These words speak to me of the deepest needs of all Christian people today, whatever their background or denomination. They hold the promise of a kind of believing that will be strong and unshakable, yet at the same time open-minded and open-hearted.

The test reminds us that Christian belief centers on the love of Christ. This love is described as something much more than a mild admiration for the person of Jesus and desire to go his way. It's called a "knowledge that is beyond knowledge." That's something we can understand better today than in the days when people thought that the knowledge we get from the five senses or from scientific experiment, is the only real knowledge we can have. Many used to be troubled by what seemed a rigid division between things we really know—that two and two make four, that the earth goes round the sun, and that a revolution happened here in 1776—and things that are simply a matter of religious belief. It seemed as if we could only guess that there may be a God, imagine that he may be interested in us, and hope there may be some kind of heaven. Some still think this way, but most realize that the situation has now entirely changed. No one can be dogmatic anymore about the certainties of science or everyday experience and the so-called speculations of religion. There is no solid atom any more to be a symbol of the sure knowledge of the material world. Scientists tell us that the origin of the universe, or its essential nature, is more like a thought, a word, a movement of the spirit, than a particle of matter. We can no longer say that the only things we really know are those that are obvious to our senses or provable by experiments.

Of course, we've really known this all along, if we stop to think about it. Most of us would claim to know something about love, truth, or beauty, just as firmly as we know the

shape of our dining room table. What man who loves his
wife would suggest that this knowledge is somehow less
valid and enduring than his knowledge that she has blue
eyes? So surely the way is open to what the New Testament says about the love of Christ. This is something we
can know, though, as the apostle says, it is beyond the
knowledge of the five senses or the operations of the mind.

To be a Christian believer is to know the God who
meets us in Jesus Christ. And this is a knowledge of his
love. We are, according to prayer, to be "strong to grasp,
with all God's people, the love of Christ, and to know it,
though it is beyond knowledge." What we should be about
in the churches is to experience this love, to reflect it, and
to share it. Nothing matters more, whatever else we may be
led to do. This is something we do together "with all God's
people." There are cults today that offer private experiences of God, or purely personal ways of salvation. And
sometimes Christianity is presented as a religious "do-it-
yourself" kit, a solo effort to reach peace of mind and
spiritual power. The New Testament offers no example of
this lone believer. "May you be able to grasp with all God's
people, the love of Christ" is the wording of the prayer.
And this chimes in exactly with the present understanding
that only in lively groups of seeking and believing people
does faith really come alive.

But it is the depth and reality of faith that matters.
That's what I like about the opening words of this prayer:
"With deep roots and firm foundations. . . ." This is the
kind of faith we are going to need in the years ahead, and
this is the kind of faith Jesus both taught and lived. He
wasn't interested in a religion that is no more than a pious
hope, or a psychological jag to keep us moderately happy.
The life he lived and the life he offers us is one of total
trust in God, one that is immersed in his love and upheld
by his grace. That means much more than an occasional
thought about him, or casual allegiance to his church. It has
roots in the Gospel of such depth and reality that nothing in
life or death can shake it. You remember how Jesus con-

trasts the house built on rock to the one built on sand.
When the tempest comes, the one stands firm while the
other collapses. Likewise, he contrasts the seed that fell on
the good ground with that which fell on the stony ground
where there is no depth. The one grew securely and yielded
abundant fruit while the other withered away because, he
said, "it had not roots."

Any one of us can swim along in times of health and
prosperity with a soft religion and a shallow faith. So can
any church, or any nation. But when the storms come, we
will know what it means to have deep roots and firm foundations. I believe, therefore, that the age we are living in
demands a strengthening and deepening of our faith, whatever our present allegiance may be. The first duty of our
church today is to offer nourishment in the faith by a proc-
lamation of the Word, a celebration of the sacraments, an
opportunity for growth and Christian education, and a supportive fellowship of Christian friends. It is a time for a
new hearing of the Word, a fresh look at prayer and meditation, a resolute grasping of the love of Christ, and a
readiness to follow the leading of the Spirit.

All this is easily said, and sounds familiar. I can almost
hear someone saying: "So what you want in the next few
decades is a return to the pieties of the past, but we've had
enough of so-called spiritual religion that makes no impact
on the world around us. Do you really want churches that
produce narrow-minded and bigoted believers who are
blind to the real questions of the day, dumb when asked to
speak about them, and chronically deaf to the music of the
arts?" In other words, it is often assumed that to be thus
rooted in what the Bible calls the love of Christ is to be
morally stunted, mentally crippled, and culturally deprived.

Listen to this prayer again: "With deep roots and firm
foundations may you be strong to grasp, with all God's
people. . . ." Is it referring to some kind of sentimental religious assurance, so we can slide through life with blinkers,
saving our own souls? No, it refers to nothing less than "the
breadth and length and height and depth of the love of

Christ. . . ." It is precisely when the roots are deep and the foundations firm that we are set free to an active exploration of the infinite dimensions of life and of God's mysterious universe. Having told us to be firmly anchored in the faith, the apostle now sends us roaming across the wide horizons of human experience with open hearts and minds. That's how I interpret these four dimensions of the love of Christ.

Think first of the breadth. Have we realized the breadth of the faith in which we are rooted? Do we understand that it's only by having firm foundations that we can truly cultivate breadth of heart and mind? There is a curious notion abroad that it is only the man or woman without firm faith who can be really broad-minded—that only one with no religious roots can be tolerant, accepting, and gracious with other people. What about Jesus? On the human level did anyone ever have deeper roots or firmer foundations of faith? What breadth there was in his teachings about the kingdom of God, his ethical insights, his vision of the world around him; and what breadth of compassion as he welcomed the outcasts, the unloved and the unlovely. It has been my experience that most of the really broad-minded and open-hearted men and women I have known have been those with deep roots and firm foundations in the love of Christ. Intellectually, there is far more breadth for the believer who leaves room for the realm of the spirit and for the eternal than for the secularist who rules them out. Emotionally there is more breadth for one who is rooted in the love of Christ than for those who have no such light to live by.

We need churches, then, with breadth to accommodate many different views within this fellowship of faith. We don't have to agree on all points of doctrine, or ways of worship—still less on the political issues of the day. And we should be prepared to listen to, and respect, those who hold some other faith, or none at all. And we should remember the breadth of that love which in Jesus welcomed every kind of person as an heir of the kingdom.

Then, there is the length. Have you ever used the expression: "I am at the end of my tether"? We are told in this prayer that there is no end to the tether that is anchored in the love of Christ. Have you ever felt like saying: "I'm at the end of my tether. I've done all I can for that person. I've tried to be kind, loving, and patient, but now I've had it"? But such is the extent or length of Christ's love that we can never be at the end of his tether. We are to be like those of whom we say, "He or she will go to any lengths to help." For that is precisely what Jesus did. With strong roots and firm foundations he went the length of crucifixion and descent into hell for us. And that is what gives the possibility of such untethered love for those who really know him.

I like to think of the Communion table in my church as having these dimensions. I see its breadth as something more than three feet and its length as something more than six. Its breadth stretches out to all who will come in faith, whatever their race, denomination, or social status. Its length stretches back to that infinite compassion of Christ, who died for us and speaks of his endless longing to give us the presence and forgiveness of the heavenly Father.

Then about the height and depth? Just as the table in my visions seems to point upward to the ultimate mysteries of the glory of God and downward to the lowest point that we can reach in our earthly struggle, so I find in the love of Christ an infinite adventure of the mind and spirit, and an unfathomable resource for living. Height and depth are symbols of that transcendent world with which we must all have to do. The height and depth of the love of Christ means for me a summons to explore the wonders of that which is beyond our ordinary knowledge. It is an invitation to open the mind to eternal horizons, and at the same time a tremendous reassurance that there is no depth of human experience, no abyss of the demonic, no hell of isolation or abandonment, from which we cannot be rescued.

I hope that something I have said—or rather, something from this Bible prayer—will reveal that firm faith and wide horizons go together. The greatest event of the next decades for our churches, and for our land, would be the emergence of a people, drawn from all sectors of the community, with deep roots and firm foundations in the love of Christ, who at the same time joyfully explore the breadth and length and height and depth of his amazing grace.

Lord, we seek the power of thy Spirit to give us deep roots and firm foundations in the love of Christ and to send us boldly out to discover more of his truth, to be more faithful in his way, and to explore the wonders of his life. Amen.

18

One Thing I Know About the Future

Do you ever have the feeling that in this age of statistics, computers, and projections we are being robbed of the unexpected? The growth of opinion polls, for instance, has made it almost impossible for us to be surprised by the results of an election. We are continually fed statistics to show us what is going to happen to the neighborhood we live in, how many babies are going to be born in the next ten years, how many people will be killed on the highways during a holiday weekend, how many couples will be divorced each year, and even what our own life-expectancy should be. It begins to seem as if we need only to provide enough data to the machines for them to forecast the future and rub out the element of surprise. Happily, we know that from time to time the machines make a slip. A last-minute swing deceives the pollsters in an election. The weathermen are notoriously something less than infallible in their forecasts. Sudden changes of opinion and habit upset statistical calculations. Still the feeling haunts us. When all these instruments are perfected, will the future really be totally predictable? What will happen to the spirit of hope, wonder, and delight in the unexpected?

If we pause for a moment to think about some of the

things that have happened in the past year, I think we'll find this specter of a human race that knows ahead of time exactly what's going to happen is easily exorcized. Which of us today really had the slightest idea that the past twelve months would bring so many changes at home and on the international scene? Have there not been in your own life some events which, by no stretch of the imagination, you could have foreseen this time last year? We begin to see that statistics and projections really deal only with trends and figures. They don't deal with persons and their mysterious freedom of choice. To say that X number of people will be killed on the roads, or die of cancer, means little. The question, "Will I, or someone I love, be one of them?" remains unanswered and unanswerable.

The Bible, you may have noticed, doesn't deal much with trends and tendencies, with round numbers and sweeping generalizations. When David was king of Israel there were such things as censuses, political predictions, and stern warnings about the consequences of war and rebellion. Poets sang about "ten thousand" falling in battle, but what the Bible dwells on is the devastating effect of unexpected tragedy on the individual. When David learned that his own rebellious son Absalom was dead, we do not read that he shrugged his shoulders and talked of the inevitability of X percent of the rebels being killed. What we hear is this: "And the king was much moved, and went up to the chamber over the gate, and wept: and as he went, thus he said, O my son Absalom, my son, my son Absalom! would God I had died for thee, O Absalom, my son, my son!" (2 Sam. 18:33). So it is with the happy moments of life. The Bible doesn't contain a book of rules and statistics governing the love life of men and women. But it does contain a book that celebrates the tempestuous, joyous, love of one man for one woman and of one woman for one man. "Behold, thou art fair, my love; behold, thou art fair; thou hast doves' eyes (Song of Sol. 1:15). . . . My beloved is mine, and I am his: he feedeth among the lilies" (Song of Sol. 2:16).

The Bible, as usual, is right. What matters is not the round figure, the average, the trend, but the human being, like you and me. And the truth still is that we do not know what is coming to us. Jesus knew that he was speaking to men and women who felt helpless as they contemplated their own future, and often worried themselves sick about the basic securities of life—health, food, and clothing. As things go today, we are perhaps closer to them than we were in days of greater affluence and stability. Yet at no time in human history could anyone be certain of total security for the future. That's not how life is. As Robert Burns put it: "The best laid schemes o' mice an' men gang aft a-gley." In one split second the whole tenor of our life can be changed. I remember once talking to an airman in World War II who had been shot down over the English Channel and found himself in the prison camp where I happened to be at the time. He told me of his daily routine of patrolling, and how on this occasion he said to himself: "There's nothing doing. I'll have one more sweep round and then I'll be home in time for lunch with my wife." Instead there he was sharing a different kind of meal with his fellow prisoners.

What Jesus had to say about this fundamental uncertainty that surrounds us as we speed into the future is still enormously potent. Much though I love the King James Version of the Bible, I realize that Jesus did not say: "Take no thought, saying, What shall we eat? or, What shall we drink? or wherewithal shall we be clothed?" He said, "Do not be anxious." He was certainly not against forethought in making provisions for the future. In fact, he often talked about the folly of carelessness and recklessness—such as the man who sets out to build a tower without reckoning carefully how much it is going to cost, or the king who rashly declares war without estimating the relative strength of his forces and the enemy's. He certainly can't be quoted as forbidding such things as making a will or taking out insurance. But he categorically rejects worry: "Be not anxious." What is being said is that we don't know what is going to happen and, therefore, anxiety is a futile frame of mind.

But Jesus was the last person to give merely negative advice. What is more irritating when we have one of these black moods about the immediate future than the cheerful advice not to worry? You can't stop anxiety by pulling a switch. Jesus supplied a reminder of the one thing that we really do know about the future—that God is there. "Don't be anxious about these things," he says, "for God knows— your heavenly Father knows that you have need of all these things" (Matt. 6:31,32). The only way to face the future without worry is to believe that God knows our real needs, and that whatever happens to us the heavenly Father will be there. The one thing I know about the future is that God knows, God cares, and he will continue to work for good with those who love him.

Like you, this confidence and trust don't come easily. I wish I could say that I have completely banished all worry and anxiety, but I haven't. But I can say that in my experience, the closer I am to God the less likely I am to fret about the future. That's why I can say that I *know* this one thing about the future. It's the kind of knowledge that grips us when we really commit ourselves to the one whom Jesus called Father. Even when fears slip in, there is still the voice that says: "I know that everything is in the hands of God, and that he wants the best for us, eternally."

There's a psalm you may remember that sings of the inescapable presence of God. "Whither shall I go from thy spirit? or whither shall I flee from thy presence? If I ascend up into heaven, thou art there. If I take the wings of the morning, and dwell in the uttermost parts of the sea; even there shall thy hand lead me, and thy right hand shall hold me" (Ps. 139:7-10). These are flaming words of faith, a faith that leaps in response to a living God who reveals that there is no corner of his universe that is off limits to his love. There is nowhere one can go where he is not already present. It's that last thought I want to stay with for a moment. The psalmist is not only saying that God is present

everywhere in space; he is also present everywhere in time.
He is not only the living God whom we may meet any-
where (there is no such thing as a Godless place, or a
Godless people), but the One who is Lord of the future, the
One of whom it can be said: Wherever you go, God is
already there.

It makes a huge difference to me when I am confident
that God is already at the very place where I may fear to
go, already waiting for me when I reach that point of difficult decision or of dark uncertainty. Do you believe that
there is any crisis looming ahead of us that is beyond the
range of God? If you read the 139th psalm again you will
find this conviction that God was there from the moment of
your conception, through all your adventures, and will be
there whatever lies ahead right through to the point of
death—and beyond.

God was there in your beginning. It was not some
fortuitous mingling of genes and chromosomes that led to
your arrival here. The astounding discoveries of biology
have nothing to say to the deeper truth that reaches us
through the music of the psalm: "Thou it was who didst
fashion my inward parts; thou didst knit me together in my
mother's womb" (Ps. 139:13). God was already there and his
grace was calling you into the kingdom of his love. From
our conception we are God's: "Thou didst see my limbs
unformed in the womb, and in thy book they are all recorded" (Ps. 139:16).

So it is through the whole tale of joy and sorrow that
makes up our human lives. He's there in our moments of
greatest joy and ecstasy: "If I ascend up to heaven, thou art
there." And there has been, and will be, no moment of
anguish where he is not to be found. "If I make my bed in
hell, behold, thou art there." Even at those times when we
soar off on our own to try to discover the illusory freedom
of life without God, he is still around. "If I take the wings of
the morning, and dwell in the uttermost parts of the sea,
even there thy hand shall lead me, and thy right hand shall
hold me" (Ps. 139:9,10). Looking back at the events of the

past months don't you recognize that God was there, even at those moments when you were not really reckoning with his presence?

There is no darkness, not even the darkness of the future, that is empty of God. The supreme moment of darkness, the worst that could ever happen in our human story, was when the sky grew black at Calvary and Jesus died. Yet there he knew, as he "made his bed in hell," that God was still there, the God to whom he commended his departing spirit, the God who would lift him from the grave. Why is it that Christians have always found, when in deepest despair or anguish, that the cross is their refuge and their strength? Isn't it that when we think of what happened there, we know that whatever we may have to pass through God has already been there. In Christ he knows all that we may have to endure, and there is nothing more to be feared. So we know that wherever we go, and whatever we may have to suffer, we shall find waiting for us the crucified and risen Lord.

That's what I know about the future—that this amazing God is there. When I know that, I am content to be agnostic about everything else that lies ahead. Indeed I am glad that no computer, no crystal ball, no soothsayer can spell it out for me. I am content with the freedom that comes with the uncertainties of our human condition when I know that it is exercised within the family of God. I don't want to know all the things that may happen to me next year, but it means everything to know that God will be there, that in fact he is there already.

Sometimes, around an area like Times Square in New York City, I have come across one of these shaggy, grim-looking characters bearing a sign that says "Prepare to meet thy God!" They are a favorite subject for cartoonists, and the assumption is that this is meant to be a terrible threat. I would like to rescue these words from this connotation. Do we really have such guilty consciences that we can only assume that such a meeting with our God would be disastrous for us? If you stop to think about it, these are splendid words. For this is the One I want to meet when my time on earth is over. The conviction that God is ahead of us wherever we go stretches out to the life immortal. Wherever we go, right to the very end, God is there already. "Even there—when the curtain falls—thy hand will meet me and thy right hand will hold me fast." Is there really anything more important to do than to prepare to meet our God. For that means strengthening here and now all those things—faith, hope, love, beauty, and truth—that partake of the eternal. That is infinitely more worthwhile than idly speculating about future events, or foolishly worrying about what may, or may not, happen. God help us to move into the unknown facing toward him.

Into thy hands, O God, we commit ourselves. Receive our thanks for all that has brought us closer to thee, and give us a sure and simple trust that the future is bright with thy presence and alive with the promise of thy grace; through Jesus Christ our Lord. Amen.